Why You Need To Read This Book

Everyone dreams of learning at least one new language, but so few of us ever accomplish this goal. Many learn a handful of words and phrases, but most struggle to learn vocabulary enough for a decent conversation. This is due entirely to a lack of vocabulary.

Why do people struggle with vocabulary? Some say they don't have time, others say it's too tough, but most say that they have a bad memory.

I used to tell myself that I have a bad memory too. Worse, when I sat in my language classes, I used to swear English words in my head that would have made my poor instructor blush. Such was my frustration with memorizing vocabulary.

My frustration increased until I finally created the unique Memory Palace tactic taught in this book. It is a set of techniques based around the Spanish alphabet that will help you acquire countless Spanish words at rapid pace. Rather than struggling to remember what used to be one or two new words a day, you can now memorize dozens of words in less than an hour using my system.

Within a month of applying myself to Spanish using the Memory Palace method described in this book, I knew the meaning and the sound of over 300 words. Within three months I could read poetry, literature and newspapers that in the past, would have sent me screaming for the dictionary.

I chose to learn Spanish after getting good at German because I made many friends from Chile and Spain while living in Berlin. Although most of them spoke both English and German, I wanted to experience their ideas and friendship in their own language. Soon, I was talking to them about music, philosophy, film, dreams of future success and many other subjects that I enjoy sharing with my Spanish-speaking friends.

Of course, the people around me quickly noticed my progress with Spanish and flocked to me for advice on how to memorize languages. My "guerilla" memory tactics are very attractive to people, especially when they realize that they help achieve near-fluency in a short period of time, assuming that they actually use the techniques and frequently converse with native Spanish speakers, either in person or using online discussion boards.

I am always pleased to help people with their desire to memorize the vocabulary of new languages. I regularly have people tell me that they have successfully memorized their first 100 words within an hour using what I teach. Make no mistake: these techniques work. They work for me, they work for everyone who has read my books and they will work for you.

I have written this book for anyone struggling to learn and memorize Spanish vocabulary. The book is designed for language learners who either want to supplement other language programs they are using, or who want to sit with a dictionary and firmly lodge every word they read in their mind for instant and accurate recall whenever they like.

There are three obstacles standing between you and memorizing massive amounts of Spanish vocabulary quickly and easily.

1. The Belief That You Don't Need A Memorization Strategy For Learning Spanish Vocabulary

Most language learners rely on rote learning. They listen to tapes that prompt them to repeat the same phrases over and over again in the hopes that the vocabulary will stick with them. Be honest. You have secretly hoped that by merely repeating a word or phrase over and over, you will retain it in your mind forever. I'm not saying that this approach doesn't work, nor am I saying that audio trainings that use repetition aren't worth your while. They most certainly are. What I am saying, however, is that the fantasy of rote learning makes many people give up because it simply does not work very well without a dedicated memorization strategy. Use and implement the techniques described in this book and you will succeed in your goal of learning Spanish vocabulary.

2. The Belief That You Can't Use Memorization Techniques

People often tell me that memorization techniques simply don't work for them. I always confidently respond by saying "yes they will." I provide a quick demonstration taught at the end of this book and discuss scholarly evidence that proves that we all have the ability to successfully memorize any amount of information we choose when we have the right strategies in place.

Richard C. Atkinson's study of the use of memory

techniques for language learning conducted at Stanford University is one of countless studies. Humorously, Atkinson calls the pen and paper many use for rote learning a "cheap memory device" that is virtually worthless in comparison to the memory techniques offered in this book.

Repeatedly writing the same word again and again is a very old technique from the time when teachers smacked their students' knuckles for misbehavior. Just as physical punishment rarely improved anyone's behavior for long, don't think that rote memorization is going to give you permanent access to the words you want to own for good.

In closing his study, Atkinson concluded that all language-learning classes include memorization techniques in their curriculum. The incredible leaps made by language learners when using memorization techniques are indisputable.

The Belief That This Business of Memorization Is Too Much Work

The memorization strategies you will find in this book take between 2-5 hours to set up. Once you've prepared the paths for yourself, the effects of the training will be immediate. The steps are so easy and fun that you'll quickly realize what a waste of time rote learning is. As soon as you've understood the memorization principles taught in this book and applied the system, you will be learning and retaining new Spanish words in a matter of seconds.

Let me make a suggestion to you before we begin: Believe in the power of your mind. I failed to believe in mine for a very long time, but now I speak, read and write German beautifully and am doing the same with Spanish, along with Russian, a language that requires but a simple extension of the system taught in this book to embrace its beautiful alphabet.

This ability to quickly memorize large numbers of words from any language has opened the doors of the world to me. Understanding another culture requires a sophisticated vocabulary and one that is not limited to phrases related to basic greetings and travel. Obviously, you can use the system taught in this book to learn and retain those phrases much better than you will with rote learning, but my goal for you is to be able to sit with a dictionary and walk away with 50-100 words lodged in your mind less than an hour later.

The best part is that with a language like Spanish, you are getting access to not just one culture, but the cultures of multiple countries. Spanish is the official language of over 14 countries. It is the de facto or legal language of another 6 countries and many other countries around the world boast substantial populations of Spanish speakers, particularly the United States and Canada.

With an advanced Spanish vocabulary, you can travel to these countries and experience them with greater intensity than you ever could have dreamed. You'll talk with people you could never have met otherwise. You'll receive service reserved for people who exhibit their care in learning the language of the country they are visiting. If you are in business, you will make deals with greater ease and efficiency, particularly if you apply what you learn in this book to memorizing how Spanish speakers use their language to persuade. You'll be able to read Spanish newspapers, enjoy movies, plays, literature and even paintings with a much deeper joy and understanding. You, like me, can and will do this. Give me 2-5 hours of your time and I will give you the techniques and abilities need to memorize all the Spanish vocabulary you want without end.

How to Learn and Memorize Spanish Vocabulary ...

Using a Memory Palace Specifically Designed for the Spanish Language

Anthony Metivier, PhD

Table of Contents

Introduction 1
Chapter 1: The Main Principles 9
Chapter 2: Applying the Main Principles 23
Chapter 3: Creating and Managing Your Spanish Language Memory Palaces 39
Chapter 4: Extending Retention Using Compounding 42
Chapter 5: Example Memory Palace for the Letter A 46
Chapter 6: Example Memory Palace for the Letter C 50
Chapter 7: Example Memory Palace for the Letter E 52
Chapter 8: Choosing the Most Important Words 55
Chapter 9: How to Use Relaxation for Vocabulary Memorization 67
Conclusion 71
About the Author 74
More Memorization Resources 75

Introduction

I learned to speak Spanish in Germany, of all places.

This took place after making the acquaintance of many people from both Chile and Spain in one of Europe's most exciting cities. When I'm not lecturing, I play bass in a band with two people from Chile and the more I came to know them, the more Spanish speakers I met. I also wanted to learn at least rudimentary Spanish because our rehearsal sessions would often slip between German, English and Spanish, leaving the singer and myself in the dust when the guitar player and the drummer, both native Chileans, started talking to one another in one of the most beautiful vocabularies I have ever heard.

Luckily, I had a great deal of experience learning German. I knew what didn't work, such as rote learning. I also knew the limits of using audio programs to accelerate my learning, particularly because these rely on repetition.

Don't get me wrong: repetition does have an effect. It's just arduous and often gets boring. Rote learning also trains the mind to not get it right the first time.
Using a memory palace, on the other hand, not only increases the chances that you'll get it right the first time. It makes it entirely possible that you'll keep the

word you've just learned *forever*.
Before I continue, let me tell you the story of how I developed my memory palace system for German. Then I will take you through all the steps of that system and then show you exactly how it can be applied to Spanish. I will teach you how to set up your 27-letter memory palace system and then give you many examples of how you can populate your palaces with Spanish vocabulary words.

Let's go back to a wonderful time in my life. I was living in Manhattan, but after nearly two years in the Big Apple, I decided I wanted to move to Berlin. But first I knew I needed at least some rudimentary German. I attended a number of lessons in a small Manhattan church in a part of the city that has been historically associated with German immigrants.
The teacher in that school played old cassettes from a learning program called *Warum Nicht?* The teacher showed maximum patience and kindness as her students struggled with the words and meanings of the German words, taking turns to repeat what we heard on the old cassettes.

I learned very little German sitting in that church. Nor did I learn very much German in Berlin. It is one of the most beautiful cities in the world and there are German speakers everywhere. I even went to class for six months, four hours a day, five days a week. My serious devotion to learning the language did not help me get the vocabulary to stick. I felt like I had a giant breach in my head, one that leaked out every new word I would learn faster than I could learn it.

Not shy of rote learning at the time, I spent hours writing out the same word over and over again. However, this did little more than hurt my wrist. At one point, I even taught myself to write with my non-dominant hand (something I recommend to anyone who wishes to increase their brain power).

Learning this new writing skill aside, it was frustrating to lose hours and hours of my time on the futile practice of rote learning. In fact, the only word I remember from my time spent rote learning is *allmählich*. This German word means, ironically, "gradually."

Fed up, I searched the Internet and libraries for a memory system designed specifically for vocabulary acquisition. I read countless books on memorization skills and listened to a large number of audio programs that I have listed in the resources section of this book. This was time well-spent because I learned a massive amount about the memory and the power of the human mind. Here and there I found language tips that were useful and will be useful for you to in future chapters. However, I failed to find anything substantial regarding how to memorize the *vocabulary* of a specific language.

Because this was my main interest, I knew I would have to develop my own method for memorizing the vocabulary of my target language, which was German at the time. I wanted a system that would allow me to place words in my mind and then instantly recognize them when I heard them spoken or read them in a book. I wanted this system to rely solely on my mind and be available to me whenever I needed. Not once did I dream that such a system would be easy to create or use, but I did believe that once placed into my mind, I would be able to use it without hassle and even enjoy working with it.

As it turns out, building and using my memory system for vocabulary acquisition has turned out to be much easier than I thought it would be and much more fun as well.

Once I had the system in place and had been using it for a while, I realized that it could be readily adapted to any other language with a little imagination. For the reasons described at the beginning of this chapter, Spanish is the language I chose next.

And now let me thank you for granting me the chance to offer my system to you. I want you to learn this unique approach by showing you the exact steps I took throughout my entire journey towards ongoing memory mastery. I want to help you understand the process in intricate detail so that when you are satisfied with your progress with Spanish and would like to try another language, you can easily adapt the system taught in this book to your own purposes.

Many of us are familiar with memory stunts. We've either seen someone on television producing long lists of numbers or recalling the names of dozens of strangers they've only just met. Many readers of this book will probably have already heard the name Harry Lorayne, if not read one of his memory books (they're excellent). However, many people find it difficult to imagine why they would want to train their brains to remember so much stuff. For other people, the idea of remembering anything and everything they would like is appeal, but it seems to them to be too much ditch-digging (i.e. hard work). Yet others tell me that the techniques I teach don't work for them.

Let me assure you that what you are going to learn in this book has nothing to do with stunts. It has nothing to do with photographic memory. We are talking about real skills that anyone can develop with a minimum amount of effort. To get really good takes practice, it's true, but the skills themselves are simple to learn and also very fun. In this book you will learn the ancient art of memory (*Ars Memorativa*) and how to apply this art to the memorization of Spanish vocabulary. As a result of your positive decision to use your memory in this way, you are going to walk away with a memory that is improved in many more ways than you could have imagined possible.

As I noted before, many people feel that memorization techniques don't work for them. This is not an attitude I accept, particularly because I used to share it. I used to love telling people about my poor memory. When we do this, we essentially train the people around us to treat us this way, which reinforces our beliefs about our inefficient memories. It is a negative cycle. I broke free by learning these skills, and the fact of the matter is that when learned and used in the correct manner, these memory techniques will change your life.

> "Like a Ten-Speed bike, most of us have gears we do not use."
> Charles Schultz

What I tell people who claim they have a bad memory is that memory techniques are like bicycles. Everyone can use them. Not everybody does, but regardless of body shape, and in many cases even with certain disabilities, there are very few of us who cannot get on a bike and ride.

But bikes have adjustable parts, and like bicycles, the memory techniques taught in this book need to be adjusted by the person using them. Just as we need to re-angle the handlebars, or lower the seat on a new bike, the memory systems taught in this book will need tweaking. Once you've understood them and started to use them, you'll find ways to suit them to your brain type (as opposed to body type).

Before we continue, I'd like you to realize that learning Spanish is rewarding for reasons that go beyond the importance of this language in the modern world. Using your memory to learn a new language is fun to do and, as a form of mental exercise, it sends oxygen rich blood to your brain, improving health and helping to prevent diseases like Alzheimer's and Dementia. But you don't have to drag yourself to the gym to achieve this. You can work out in your favorite armchair, while driving or sitting at the beach. You can develop your memory wherever you happen to be and practice Spanish with ease because you'll have every word you've learned perfectly organized within the work-out gym of your mind.

When it comes to learning and memorizing Spanish vocabulary, there is no other book like this out there. A word of caution: although it will take until the final chapters before we get into the memory palace construction work and start placing our Spanish vocabulary words with these new palaces, please don't flip past the other pages in this book. I have written them to train you in the basics, help you become advanced and give you countless valuable ideas for how to adjust the ancient techniques of memory for your own purposes. I will show you things I had tried that didn't work for me, but may work for you. And I will show you how I have adjusted the techniques in ways that made them more workable.

Much of this book is written in a conversational style, but each chapter ends with a set of action steps that you can use to begin implementing the techniques immediately. The final chapters give you plenty of examples of how I work with the palaces to memorize words so you model how the system works in detail.

I normally don't wish my students and readers good luck because my goal is to give them tools and skills that make luck irrelevant. I wrote this book so that your storage and retrieval of Spanish vocabulary words is instantaneous, fun and easy and created in a way that you can apply it to any other language you choose to tackle. No, luck, or la fortuna won't be necessary. But ... I take that back. Let me wish you good luck anyway. ¡Buena suerte!

Chapter 1: The Main Principles

There are three main principles involved in what I call "memory amplification." I use this term because memory techniques do seem to "turn up the volume." This means that the memory palaces themselves become kind of like storage units for our roaring Spanish words.

The three principles we will learn in this chapter are: **location**, **imagery**, and **activity**. Along with these principles, we have **Preparation** and **Predetermination.** Let's look at each of these in turn. Keep in mind that each of principles is individually important and each are interrelated. Use them independently, and they will still help improve your memory. Use them together and your memory skills will soar beyond belief.

If you are interested in the history of memory techniques, I highly recommend reading this webpage: http://www.mundi.net/cartography/Palace. Joshua Foer's recent book *Moonwalking with Einstein: The Art and Science of Memory* is also fantastic, but please be advised that this book covers more cultural history than specific guidance when it comes to building memory palaces for language acquisition. But if you're serious about improving your memory in ways that will directly impact your ability to learn Spanish, then you have everything to gain by reading all that you can on the topic.

Location

Location is part of, but not the entire picture of the memory palace concept. Locations are used to store imagery. The reason we use locations is because we tend to remember places we've been without exerting any effort, and this is one of the key principles of memory work: eliminate everything that you don't have to work at remembering and build natural associations.

When thinking about locations for storing memories, try doing something that I did for myself. I once determined that I have lived in eight cities, twenty-five houses (or apartments) and sixteen neighborhoods within those cities. I have yet to count all the houses I remember that belong to my friends and extended family members, but surely the number is exponential, because it gets expanded all the time.

There are even hotel rooms that I remember very well in cities that I have visited. The path I took from an apartment in Paris to the Louvre, for instance, has served me very well over the years.

We all have more territory in our minds than we could ever possibly hope to use for storing memories. The best part is that we can then sub-divide locations into individual stations. So if you consider an apartment a "location," then each individual room will be a station within that location.

As I'm going to discuss further on, I like to combine indoors and outdoors locations, places that I know very well. There are some advanced ways that I use imaginary locations as well, and I will teach you these in a future chapter. I think you'll be impressed by the power of location in storing memories. However, for memorizing Spanish vocabulary effectively, I suggest that you always use locations you are familiar with. It can't be said enough: the more you use places you already know, the less you have to remember.

Again, the less you have to remember, the more you can associate. And the more you can associate, the more you can remember. It's an awkward equation, I know, but it works.

By the end of this book, all will become clear, and if you're following along with the exercises, you will have already used this strange principle of pre-remembered locations to acquire at least two more languages.

But for now, let's move on to ...

Imagery

Imagery is ... well, imagery. Mental pictures that you build in your mind. For the purposes of memorization, these pictures need to be big and colorful. The larger and the more colorful, the better. Essentially, you want to exaggerate the size and colors because that will make the image more memorable. This will in turn strengthen the association. Some of the students I've taught tell me that they are not particularly visual in their imaginations and I completely understand this. In fact, when I read a novel, I rarely see images in my mind. It's always conceptual. It's possible that I have something called *Imagination Deficit Disorder* or

IDD.

Whether I suffer this condition or not, because I have a low visual threshold in my mind, I am able to give my non-visual students a few suggestions based on my own experiences.

First, if you can't think in color, don't force it. However, try thinking in black and white, taking care to exaggerate the black and white. How black is the black and how white is the white? Is there an opportunity to use gray in some memorable way?

Whatever happens, do not allow a lack of imagination for intense imagery to be a barrier. I know that you can incorporate imagination into your memory work, because as I mentioned, I am not particularly visual myself. This surprises people a great deal because I have spent a great deal of my career teaching Film Studies. I teach theory and concepts, however, and am absolutely lost when anyone asks me about how individual shots are composed.

In the event that neither color nor black and white patterns are not useful for you, another tactic, one that I have used to great effect, is to associate certain prefixes with actors or fictional characters. For instance, the Spanish prefix *cachi-* is associated in my mind with Charles "Chachi" Arcola, who was played by Scott Baio on the popular television series, *Happy Days*. The words don't sound exactly the same, but I am able to visual Chachi and make the association *cachi*. Thereafter, ever word that begins with *cachi* gets automatically linked with Chachi.

Another option is to use paintings that you are familiar with in your imagery. The more you are aware of their intricacies, the better. The next time you are in an art gallery or looking through an art book, pay closer attention to what you are looking for. The material could become fodder for better associations with the Spanish vocabulary you will be memorizing.

I must mention a small problem with artwork, however. Paintings and statues tend to be static. They don't move. That said, if you can imagine the Mona Lisa walking like an Egyptian outside of her frame, or Michelangelo's David doing the Moonwalk, then you should have no problem. Finally, you could use toys that you remember. GI Joe, Barbie, My Little Pony … anything goes. As with paintings, the most important factor here is that you can put these figures into action.

So without further adieu, let's turn our attention to …

Action

By now, you will have thought about different locations you are familiar with, sub-locations or stations within those locations and different ways that you can use exaggerated imagery.

The next step is to give your images a bit of movement. More than a bit, actually. Just as you want to exaggerate the size and color of your images, you also want to exaggerate their actions.

It's not an entirely nice way to think of things, but something that will work wonders for you is to make the action violent. Highway accidents serve as the perfect example of how memorable scenes of violence can be – even in their aftermath. If after seeing an accident or accident site you could not shake the memory of your mind, then you know how powerful violent images can be.

This is not to suggest that lives need to be lost. Cartoon violence will work just as well. Wile E. Coyote, for instance, provides a strong example of someone willing to savage himself in some pretty hilarious ways when trying to make the Road Runner his dinner.

Again, the object is to create something so potently memorable that working hard to recall the image is unnecessary. It will instantly come to mind when you look for it because you've given yourself no other choice. You've made the image impossible to forget.

Now, you may be thinking that using this technique is going to lead to a brain cluttered with bizarre images. This may happen in the beginning when you are first learning the techniques. With practice, however, the images you have used will ultimately fall away. You'll still wander your palaces and have a hankering of what the images were that you used, but they will be secondary. The word and its meaning will be the central artifact on display.

Preparation and Predetermination

Like the memory palace system itself I'll be revealing later on, Preparation and Predetermination are two memory skills that I have not seen talked about in any other memory book. I feel that both of these are essential elements to memorization success, be it a language or anything else you might like to remember.

Preparation, to begin, involves relaxing the mind. I will share several thoughts about it in the concluding chapter, but for now, please realize that when the mind is tense, busy or exhausted, it will resist attempts at memorization. This does not mean that you won't be able to remember anything. It only means that your mind won't be in the most receptive state possible. When your mind is open and relaxed, you'll be amazed by how these techniques will double, triple and even quadruple in effectiveness.

Predetermination, on the other hand, involves charting out the memory locations and stations in your memory palace system *before* making any single attempt to place the words you want to memorize. I must stress that before populating your memory palaces for Spanish, you will to have built the entire system first. Having tried to make up my palaces as I went along, I can tell you that this leads to little more than frustration and impoverished results. Please spend the necessary time to predetermine the locations that you want to use and label the individual stations within them.

Before continuing, I want to stress that perfection is not the goal here. It's important not to harm your forward movement by being too particular about every little detail. You just want to get the basic layout in place so that you can work relatively quickly with the words you want to memorize. After I have taught you the entire system, I have an entire chapter for your with recommended words and phrases that I have found the most useful to have. I will also give you samples of how I memorized those words so that you can model the procedure on your own.

Preparing Your First Location

It helps a great deal to draw a map of the locations you will be using and have some system for labeling the individual stations. Alternatively, you can list them in a Word document or catalog them in an Excel file. Some students I've had like to actually draw the different rooms or use computer architectural programs to create digital layouts.

Although I personally don't go that far, I tend to do all three of the former in order to maximize the strength of the associations I'll be making. Let's face it: If I'm going to spend time learning a language, I want the vocabulary to stay in my head. Learning grammar is pointless if you haven't got plenty of words to fit into the equations.

The first Memory Palace I ever created was my first apartment in Berlin. It had 8 stations, though I now recommend and always make sure a new memory palace I've started has at least 10.

This particular apartment was on the Feurigstraße, which means "fiery street." The name came from the fact that a fire station was located just a few blocks north of me, but that was fine because the firemen had the lovely habit of only turning the sirens on after they had left the street.

I don't mention this to be cute. All of these details come in very handy when it comes to building Memory Palaces.

First, because the apartment was on Feurigstraße, I use that apartment and every station in that palace to remember words that begin with the letter 'F.' I could use this apartment for any other letter, but this is the association that came to me naturally, and I think it is best to allow for such natural associations. Because I don't have to spend any time remembering that all 'F' words are connected with the Feurigstraße palace, I don't have to make any odd leaps. If I was placing 'S' words there, then it would take my mind a step to search for which palace has 'S' in it.

Don't worry. I'm going to go into greater detail about all of this later. But for now, the basic principle is that every location is a Memory Palace and as much as possible, that location should start with the same letter of the words that you will store there.

The Feurigstraße apartment had a nice layout:

1. My Office
2. Laundry Room
3. Bathroom
4. Bedroom
5. Wife's office
6. Living Room
7. Hallway
8. Kitchen

Later, I extended this palace outside of the apartment:

9. Outside of the door
10. Stairwell
11. Front door
12. Parking garage
13. Sidewalk
14. Used book store
15. Playground
16. Fire station
17. Church
18. Sushi restaurant

… and so forth

There are two important points that I need to mention here. In creating these "journeys" through the stations of my Memory Palace, it's important that you structure things in such a way that you:

a) Never cross your own path
b) Never trap yourself

If, when you are rehearsing your words or searching for them you have to cross your own path, you are liable to confuse yourself. It is best to create a journey that follows a straight line. With greater practice, this will become less necessary, but in the beginning stages, please keep this important point in mind.

Second, it is important that you don't trap yourself. The reason I was able to add more stations to my 'F' Memory Palace so easily is because I started at a terminal point in the apartment: my office. Had I started in the kitchen and moved toward my office, I would have trapped myself – unless I wanted to jump off the small balcony and down onto the street. Doing so would be entirely possible, but it is unnatural and causes the mind unnecessary work. Although you will be exaggerating shapes, colors and actions in your memory work, I feel that it is best to keep the movement you make through the palaces as natural as possible.

Try this out for yourself. Describe the layout of the place you live in now and make a list of at least 10 individual stations. You can make a handmade list or use an Excel file. There is good reason to get started with Excel files right away for the purposes of testing the strength of your memorizations.

Decide upon what letter your current palace will be used to represent. Make sure that you choose well, and realize that because Spanish has one letter more than English, after this one is set, you're going to need 27 more. There are only a very few words that start with ñ, but you're going to want to have a palace for them nonetheless.

For now, here are some actions steps that will help you master the techniques taught in this chapter. Please get started immediately.

> 1. Select at least 10 different locations that you remember well. If you are feeling motivated, you can readily list all 27. These could be apartments or houses you've lived in, schools, libraries, workplaces or art galleries. All that matters is that you know them

well and can walk around them in your mind. I find that multi-screening room movie theatres work really well for me, and as a film professor, I have over a dozen theatres that I am intimately familiar with.
2. Select and list at least 10 "stations" within each of the locations you listed. These different stations will become the places you will leave each of the words you want to memorize within each palace. These stations can be entire rooms, which I recommend when you are just getting started, or they can be more specific. You could use an armchair and then the lamp table beside it as two different stations, for instance. Even though you will not need to remember any of these individual stations (that's the whole point), you should still write them down for the purpose of testing the strength and rigor of your memorizations.
3. Take a walk through each palace and the stations that you have identified. While wandering, make each and every station vivid in your mind. You can imagine cleaning everything out if you like, removing all the dust and dirt that can get in the way of your memorization process.
4. Draw maps. Creating visual representations of each location and the stations within them can be very powerful and save you a lot of testing time later. You definitely don't want to be vague about what comes next in your Memory Palaces. Again, using an Excel file is also a great idea if you are not a visual person, though doing both is highly recommended.
5. Practice remembering trivial things where there is no pressure if you make mistakes. The top ten highest mountains or largest rivers make for great practice.

Shopping lists also make for good practice. Remember to make everything large and colorful.

6. Include action. Let's say you're trying to remember that you need carrots on your shopping list. Imagine that you are jumping on the carrot and hurting it badly. You can use whatever image comes to your mind, so long as it is over-the-top, hilarious, zany and memorable. If you relax, you'll find that your mind will come up with material very naturally.

7. On that point, always practice in a state of relaxation. I have included specific notes on the best relaxation techniques for memorization in the final chapter. These relaxation practices are also good for any form of creativity.

8. Make sure that you are having fun. When you start out practicing with memory items that have no consequence, you enable yourself to play freely with the concept. If you start with Spanish vocabulary right away, you risk associating frustration and the occasional failure with the language you've always dreamed of learning. Make sure that you can memorize at least ten items you know nothing about before attempting any words. And of course, read the rest of this book too so that you have plenty of examples to guide you.

9. Give yourself an exam. As I've stressed, you really need to write everything down for the purposes of testing. This is not rote learning. It's a method of giving you the ability to double check. Also, when testing, don't look at the original list you created. Write out everything fresh and then compare the list you wrote out from memory with the original.

10. Teach. The best way to truly learn a technique is to teach it to someone else. You should discuss your newfound knowledge about memorization as often as possible because this will deepen your familiarity with the techniques and prove to yourself and others that these things really do work. It's not showing off to do so. You'll also be making the world a better place because you'll be enabling others to use their minds more effectively. Make working on your own memory and helping others improve theirs a habit for life.

Chapter 2: Applying the Main Principles

This chapter explains the complete system for creating and using your 27-letter Memory Palace system. By this time, you've already created 10, if not more location palaces and charted them out either on paper or using an Excel file. You've also identified at least 10 stations within those 10 locations.

Here's how I work whenever setting myself up to memorize the essential vocabulary I will need to operate in a new language.

First, I create a folder and then create multiple Excel files. Excel works the best because it eliminates the need to build a table. However, you can just as easily build a table using Microsoft Word, Pages or whatever Word Processing software you happen to be using.
In this case, the files you need to create correspond to the following letters (in the following example, I tell you what my selected locations for Spanish happen to be):

A = Aberdeen Mall
B = Brandonhurst Elementary School
C = Carpet World
D = Maintstreet Downtown
E = Eric's House

F = Feurigstraße
G = Dad's Garage
H = Hospital
I = Ice Rink
J = Jasmine's House
K = Kirk's House
L = Lyle's House
M = Manny's House
N = Nolene's House
Ñ = Natalie's House
O = Olympic Stadium
P = Philipinnenstraße
Q = Quinn's House
R = Rick's House
S = Sahali Mall
T = Trevor's House
U = University Library
V = Varsity Movie Theatre
W = Wicklow Movie Theatre
X = Kane's House
Y = Yorkville Movie Theatre
Z = Zara's House

It is very important that you have at least 10 stations assigned to each of the Memory Palaces you have selected based on locations that you are very familiar with.

Remember, design your passage from station to station in such a way that you do not cross your own path and so that you do not trap yourself. You always want to leave yourself with the ability to add another 10 stations in each location, the implication being that you may need up to 500 for some of the letters in order to achieve fluency in Spanish.

As you are trying to come up with each location to link with each letter, let yourself relax. Your mind has the perfect associations for you, so long as you don't force it. If you can't think of something that is totally fitting, such as Wicklow for W, just let your mind do its work and go with whatever feels right.

You do not want odd or awkward associations that cause you to stumble in your thinking. You want the associations to be natural so that you can move fluidly through your mind when searching for the words you have remembered. When it comes to speaking and understanding what you hear, you will sometimes need to do this in real time, so it is very important not to hinder yourself by using forced associations that you will forget and struggle to work your way back to. That will take the fun out of everything.

Now, let me show you how I have used just two letters: A and E.

For A, which is Aberdeen Mall, my first ten stations are:
1. Entrance
2. Jewelry store
3. Bookstore
4. Escalator
5. Food court
6. Shoe store
7. Grocery store entrance
8. Movie theatre entrance
9. Mall Exit

10. Parking lot

The first "A" word I would like to learn is perhaps the most important: amar. Amar means to love.

To remember that "amar" means love, I place the famous magician Michael Ammar at the entrance to the mall. I imagine him large and colorful, and perhaps rather strangely (which is the point), he is pulling a beating heart from his magician's hat. The heart itself is large and colorful and pounding away. In fact, as it beats, I hear the sound "amar" over and over again.

Next, inside the mall, I want to place "ayudar," which means to help. Since Michael Ammar worked so well for "amar," I will recruit him for the rest of the words in this palace. This is a very good trick. It is part of compounding the associations, something I will talk about in a future chapter.

"Ayudar" has a strong "you/joo" sound in it, so I need to think about how to get an image from this. For whatever reason, YouTube comes instantly to mind, so I start to get an image of Ammar punching a laptop, one that is showing a video of Yoda helping Luke Skywalker cross a street that happens to be on the surface of the Death Star from *Star Wars*.

I want you to notice something here: I've been compressing a lot of images into a single space. They are vibrant and ridiculous to me, which means that they'll be memorable. However, reflecting upon them, I realize that I don't need YouTube, because "Yoda" gives me the sound I need just as well as YouTube. And Yoda can be further compressed with the Death Star, which helps me get the "dar" sound in "Ayudar."

My point here is that as you work on developing your associations, do not hesitate to refine them. Adding on is just as important as taking away when it comes to the art of memory.

So in my final image, I have Ammar punching Yoda as he is trying to help Ammar cross a street on the Death Star. I'll have this image for as long as I want it and have "ayudar" as well.

One more example from the letter A Memory Palace. Let's learn the word for "to learn." It is "aprender." As it happens, the bookstore is the perfect place to put this word (you'll often find nice little coincidences when you do memory work).

You will sometimes get words that are tricky like this. "Pren" brings nothing to mind other than a wren with a pen in its mouth. I don't like this, however, because the image meant to trigger the "P" sound comes after the image meant to give me "ren." (I automatically know that the word starts with "A" because it is stored in my "A" Memory Palace, further compounded by the fact that Michael Ammar is going to be in the picture just as soon as I can figure out how to fit him in).

What I eventually decide to do with "aprender" is to have Michael Ammar "apprehended" by the police in front of the bookstore. Why? Because he is trying to steal of a copy of *How to Learn and Memorize Spanish Vocabulary*!

As always, I make everything huge and colorful and generally larger than life. The police are big and brutish in their blue uniforms and light sparkles from their badges, handcuffs and guns.

Please note that "aprender" can also be used for "to memorize," but the normal word for that in Spanish would be "memorizar."

What About Memorizing Grammar?

This book does not purport to teach the memorization of grammar. However, I do have a few tips for the conjugation of verbs. This involves creating a special palace just for grammar rules.

So far we have been dealing with Spanish verbs. This is where things can get tricky because you add a different ending to the verb depending on the gender and or number of people speaking.

Take, for instance, the place that I use for conjugating verbs: the school where I teach. I use the kitchen, my office, the third classroom, the computer lab, the main hall, the second classroom, the reception desk, the first classroom, the front door, the outside hall, and the staircase (it's a small school). This school is particularly appropriate for me to use because my colleague who owns it is from Argentina and is a native Spanish-speaker.

Notice here that I have started in the kitchen because it is in the very back of the school. This way, I can move in a more-or-less straight line through the school without ever crossing my path or becoming trapped. Should I want to add more information to this particular palace, I have created it in such a way that I simply need to step out the door, walk past the veterinarians, the sun-tanning salon, the barbers, the dry cleaners, etc.

Before I describe how I use this particular palace to help

remember grammar rules, let's take a brief look at verb conjugation in Spanish.

"Hablar," the word for "speak" usually appears first in most language trainings.

If you want to say "I speak," you need to conjugate the word to "hablo."

If you want to say "You speak," you need to conjugate the word to "hablas."

Likewise, "he speaks" and "she speaks" becomes "habla." "We speak" needs "hablamos." "They speak" becomes "hablan." If you are referring to men or a group with men in it, you use "ellos hablan." If the group consists of women only, the term is "ellas hablan."

Let's apply this to "aprender."

I learn = aprendo (yo aprendo)
You learn = aprendes (tú aprendes)
He learns = aprende (el aprende)
She learns = aprende (elle aprende)
We learn = aprendemos (nosotros aprendemos)
They learn = aprendéis (vosotros aprendéis)
They learn = aprenden (ellos aprenden)

To remember that "I" usually ends with "o," I see myself in the kitchen jumping up and down on a box of cheerios.

To remember that "you" words usually end with either "as"

or "es," I see myself pinning the tail on a donkey in my office.

To remember that "he" and "she" normally end with an "eh" sound, I see a Canadian saying, "What's up, eh!" in classroom number 3. He has a huge bottle of beer in his hand, and this itself says "eh" on it.

To remember that "we" usually ends with "os," I see myself with a group of students in the computer lab. "We" are marveling at the operating system on a new computer the school has purchased. It has a huge OS on the screen that is bursting with light to the point that it is burning our eyes.

To remember "they learn" is aprendéis/aprenden I have a dais in the hallway. This makes the hallway look a bit like a lecture hall, but it works. There is a lectern on the dais which says "the end" on it. This combined set of images worked marvelously when I was first trying to master this material.

Gendered Nouns

When it comes to gendered nouns, Spanish uses feminine and masculine indicators. "El" is used in singular form for masculine nouns and "los" for plural masculine nouns. "La" is feminine singular and "las" is the plural version.

Whenever you learn a new noun and place it in your memory palace, it is important that you immediately memorize its gender.

This is easily done.

I associate all masculine nouns with a boxer and all feminine nouns with a skirt.

For example, to remember that "fruta" (fruit) is feminine and therefore "la fruta," I see a pineapple wearing a skirt.

To give you an example of a masculine noun, take "el tranvía" (tram or streetcar). It's a simple matter to see a boxer fighting a streetcar. In reality, a man would be no match for such a vehicle, but in my memory palace, he is pounding the streetcar to a pulp.

The beautiful thing about taking care to associate every noun with its masculine or feminine signature is that you've already given yourself the basis for a crazy image.
There are some other words where the endings do not change depending on the person you are referring to.

"Amante" means lover, for instance, so there is no need to use a boxer or a skirt. You just ad "el," "los," "la" or "las" depending on the gender or the person or group of people you are speaking to. A group with both men and women will receive the masculine assignments.

For a fuller understanding of Spanish grammar rules, see the resources section at the end of this book.

Another Method for Storing Gender

To be as complete as possible, here's an idea I have heard

several people talk about. This procedure has never worked for me, because I find it too messy. However, that does not mean you won't find a way to use it.

Instead of having gender nouns stored in palaces based around the alphabet, some people pick a city and use it as one large Memory Palace. They then divide the city into two parts: masculine and feminine (or in the case of a language like German, into three parts to include neutral noun assignments).

Conclusion

To conclude this chapter, here is a list of action steps for immediate implementation on your journey toward memorizing Spanish vocabulary:

1. Don't do anything until you've fully and clearly understood how to use location, imagination and action in order to effectively memorize at least ten items.
2. Take your time creating the individual locations and stations within the locations. It will take between 1-5 hours to come up with 27 locations and at least 10 stations within each location, but you can speed up the process by being relaxed while you create. Your mind has everything that you need, so long as you can push your critical mind aside and let your creative mind work. Please realize that it is not absolutely necessary to devise all 27 palaces straight away. I prefer that my memory students have them set up in advance so that they are ready to pop new words in without thinking about it, but I know that some people want to focus more selectively on just the letters A through H, and that is perfectly fine too.
3. Ensure that your journey in each and every Memory Palace can be undertaken without crossing your own path or getting trapped. It is tempting to think that one can get away with circling around the forward trajectory of a path, but in the long run, this will only confuse matters. Strive for clear, crisp and direct journeys so that you don't need to think about what

belongs where. Remember, the fewer things you have to remember, the easier it will be to recall the Spanish words you've placed in your palaces.
4. Use Word or Excel or a handwritten document for each Memory Palace. Start with the first location and proceed linearly from there. Don't forget that the purpose of this part of the process is twofold. First, preparing a written record will help you build your memory palaces with much greater detail than doing it in your imagination alone. Second, your written record will allow you to test the words you have placed in your mind.
5. Examine the grammatical variations of the words you've chosen to place in your palace. Will you need to remember the gender? Is it a verb that will need declension? Allow your imagination to take the principles you have been learning from this book show you the best imagery for memorizing these different structural elements of any given word. Use relaxation to facilitate the process.
6. At the risk of being repetitive, please make sure that you are using the location, imagination and action principles. I mentor many people and a significant number of them report or demonstrate that they've fallen back on rote learning. They are repeating the words to themselves again and again rather than engaging the system I've taught them. Believe it or not, but both the mind and the body find this very stressful, contributing to fight or flight responses, frustration and ultimately failure. Future chapters describe a number of supplementary exercises that you can use to train your memory in greater depth if

you feel that you need more training. I can tell you that if I hadn't gone through those exercises myself, I never would have devised the 27-letter Memory Palace system in the first place, let alone developed any skill with acquiring a second and third language. They may not seem related, but think of it as the relationship between push-ups and boxing. Pushing the floor away from the body is one of the best ways to strengthen your punch, even though it's a completely different movement.

7. Learn the genders of every word right away. Decide upon what will signify masculine and feminine and use them consistently. This will become second nature. You don't have to use a boxer and a skirt. Go with whatever your imagination brings to you naturally.

8. Decide upon a focus. I recommend that you make adjectives a priority. Nouns and verbs are great and you will need them, but adjectives allow you to flavor your speaking and deepen your understanding of innuendo and metaphor. When you do work with verbs, pick strong verbs and learn more than one version of each (instead of just "run," also learn "jog" and "sprint"). As for nouns, use a Visual Dictionary to find your words. This will help you be more selective in the words you choose and give your imagination more fodder for making memorable associations.

9. Sit with a dictionary as often as possible. When you have worked out your 27-letter Memory Palaces in advance, you are literally going to siphon the dictionary into your mind. Although many words may fail to capture your interest, there is no need to fight

with them. Simply find the words that interest you the most or that you think will be the most useful and focus on them. Even if you skip a dozen words in a row, you can always go back to them. Focus on steady progress rather than being a completionism. Never allow frustration to enter the picture.

10. Many words you will encounter can mean several things at once. Focus on just one meaning at a time. You can always go back to gather more meanings (see the chapter on compounding).

11. Go to the library, Netflix, YouTube or a store that sells DVDs and stock up on Spanish-language programs. You are going to be amazed and proud of yourself by all the words you'll already be able to recognize and inspired to keep going and memorize more. You can still watch the films with the English subtitles on, or even better, watch them with Spanish subtitles or Spanish closed-captioning on. Mixing Memory Palaces with as much immersion as possible will make for great strides in your learning. Likewise, you can listen to Spanish audiobooks, read Spanish comics, seek out bilingual editions of famous Spanish-language novels (like *Don Quixote*) and listen to Spanish-language music. There are endless possibilities and you'll be glad that you have taken this extra step.

12. Be careful that the images you use actually help you remember the meanings of the words. It's a painful experience to have installed familiarity with the sound and spelling of a word, only to forget what it means. It's one thing to remember that "ayudar" has something to with YouTube and Yoda in your

Memory Palace, but if you can't remember that it means "to help," then time, effort and energy has been lost. Please see the following chapter on compounding for additional ideas on how to make sure that you never forget the meanings of the words you have learned.

Chapter 3: Creating and Managing Your Spanish Language Memory Palaces

Spanish vocabulary is the most rapidly acquired by learners who are prepared with the necessary number of Memory Palaces. We've already talked about some of the points covered in this chapter, but I want to devote a special section to creating and maintaining the palaces in order to add depth and detail to the process.

Every location you have identified should have at least 10 stations ready to be populated with the association-rich images that will bring the words you have learned easily to mind. You should have created the palace in such a way that you will never cross your own path or reach a dead end. You always want to be able to add more stations. It is unlikely that you will ever need more than 100 in any given palace, but if ever you do, be prepared to have places to add them.

Some people tell me that it is impossible for any given palace to have so many stations. However, if you think of all the places you've lived, it will quickly become clear to you that the possibilities are endless. If you can squeeze just 10 stations out of your current home by using individual rooms and doorways, then with a little thought, you can extend that to twenty. How do you walk to the bus stop? Surely there are numerous memorable locations on the way: the bakery, the florist, the dental clinic above the hearing loss centre. If you take the subway, each stop can become it's own station where you leave an image. For years I have used both the Toronto, New York and Berlin subway systems as Memory Palaces and each provide countless stations where I leave words that I want to remember for easy recall.

Remember: *preparing and predetermining your locations and stations in advance is of the utmost importance when it comes to rapidly acquiring a large vocabulary. Please spend the time creating your constellation of palaces before placing even a single word of Spanish vocabulary in your mind.*

The next matter of importance is relaxation. Please see the final chapter for information about that.

Next is the matter of maintenance. At the risk of being repetitive, I have included this information twice in this book. The Spanish alphabet has 27 letters. Our months have either 29, 30 or 31 days in them. This means that you will always have plenty of time for rehearsal.

Although your memorization of the vocabulary has lasting power, it is important to perform "quality control." This means revisiting the words you have memorized at least once a month. It's easy enough to do: you know where you keep all your words beginning with the letter A, so it's just a matter of wandering through the palace.

I schedule monthly maintenance sessions loosely based on the number of palaces. Take November, which has 30 days. Day 1 is dedicated to the letter A, Day 2 to the letter B and so forth. If there is a letter with a large number of words I have memorized (some of my letter palaces have 100-200), I assign more than I day to wandering through those particular palaces. Doing this is well worth the effort and it also strengthens your familiarity with the language because you can begin to see patterns and the interconnectedness of the Spanish language.

Chapter 4: Extending Retention Using Compounding

This chapter will be useful for anyone memorizing Spanish vocabulary, but especially for those who need to learn the language for purposes other than pleasure. Many professionals, particularly in the United States, learn Spanish for business purposes or for work. Without true passion behind the enterprise, even the simple technique of using memory palaces can seem drab and unexciting. There is hope and this chapter will put you in control of how you approach your memorization sessions.

Generating Excitement

In one of his information products devoted to helping people optimize their mental processes, Mike Koenigs talks about speed-reading. For him, one of the best methods for reading a book quickly is to pretend that you will be interviewing the author on live television the next day. Millions of viewers will be watching, which means that you'll need to know the book very well, with both depth of understanding about the message and accuracy about the specific details of the content.
I think Koenigs' idea is brilliant and very adaptable to memorizing Spanish vocabulary. When I am heading to events, parties or professional opportunities where I know I will need more vocabulary on hand in order to maximize the potential benefits of the occasion, I create urgency and

excitement by pretending that *I* am going to be interviewed.

I pretend that I have a book to sell that has been translated Spanish and know that people are only going to want to own it forever if I am able to win their hearts by speaking to them intelligently. To amp things up, I sometimes pretend that a movie deal is in the works, but only if I can convince the producer that I know enough Spanish to consult on the screenplay and production.

There are many motivational tricks like this that anyone can use to get themselves excited if they don't naturally feel motivated to learn and memorize Spanish vocabulary.

Compounding

When revisiting your words, you will sometimes discover that you cannot perfectly recall certain words and their meanings. You feel sure that your images are vibrant, well-located and buzzing with action and energy. Yet, when you look for the words, you still struggle to recall them.

This clambering can lead to stress and anxiety because you know that without being able to call them to mind easily and effortlessly, you are going to be self-conscious about struggling when speaking or taking a test and the thought of stress alone will make you even more self-conscious. Relax. Refuse to be frustrated or concerned because this is simply an opportunity to compound your memorizations. Many of my students feel that they want to replace the original images they've created, but I caution against this because that can leave "fossils" that will only confuse matters later.

Instead, add to the image and enhance it. Take the following example: If you, like me, use Yoda helping Michael Ammar across the street even though he's been beating the YouTube screen, but still cannot produce "ayudar," then you need to compound the image by either making it more vivid in your mind or adding something. Perhaps Ammar has "help" tattooed on his forehead, or better yet, is screaming for help because someone is branding the word "help" on his forehead. There is always a way to compound your images to make them more memorable.

Please realize that there is nothing wrong with your mind or your memory if you find weaknesses in your new 27-letter Memory Palace system. It's just a matter of compounding the images.

In addition, you might like to compound and reinforce the Memory Palaces themselves. If your memory of some of the locations you are using is not as strong as you originally thought, then you might want to work with another one. This happened to me recently when I wanted to use my old senior high school. I did my preparatory work and predetermined 20 separate stations. However, when placing new words, I found that I kept forgetting the next station.

This lack of familiarity became such a barrier that I needed, not to scrap the palace, but use it for another letter. I chose K because there are only a handful of words that begin with that letter and I could place them in a part of the palace that I definitely knew very well.

Ultimately, the amount of time you spend on rehearsing, compounding and "renovating" depends on your level of experience and general enthusiasm for memorization. Again, however, do make sure that you do your preparation and predetermination exercises as fully as possible because giving them your full attention will save you plenty of time and sweat later. But when leaks in the system do occur, no stress. Simply wander through your palaces and fix them.

Chapter 5: Example Memory Palace for the Letter A

I was once blessed with living down along a forest road. I'm not sure why my mind selected this house for the letter C, but I always think it best to go with whatever comes naturally. As I spent over a decade living there, my mind is very familiar with the location and it is therefore easy to through and chart out a number of locations for placing Spanish vocabulary words.

Here are some of the stations, the words I have placed there and a description of the images I used to learn and memorize the words. But first, I should explain that when doing memory work within a palace, I often like to group words together, at least when beginning with a new language.
In the examples that follow, I am focusing only on words that begin with "al." This helps me use a famous figure to structure my journey through the various locations. The figure I use for "al" words is Weird Al Yankovic. I chose him because he is already strange and memorable.
These examples include some rather weak entries. I've done this so that you can better see how the principle works and get a strong feel for what doesn't work and why it doesn't work.

Main bedroom: las alas [A-las]. Alas is a feminine noun that means wing. I see Weird Al, dressed in a skirt, plucking off one of Tinkerbelle's wings, both of them shouting "alas!"

Bathroom: la alberca [al-BER-ka]. Alberca is the Spanish word for pool. It is a feminine noun. In the bathroom I see a huge iceberg in the tub, which is now shaped like a pool. Weird Al, still wearing a skirt, is giving it a karate chop with his hand. As in the old Batman cartoons, "Al! Ber! Ka!" is shooting out of the action in bright and exuberant colors.

Laundry room: la alcancía [al-kan-SEE-a]. Alcancía means bank, as in the place you keep your money. The first thing that comes to mind is Weird Al playing peek-a-boo with a baby in the dryer who is tumbling around with loads of cash. The dryer looks an awful lot like a bank vault inside. Al, again wearing a skirt, is opening and closing the door rapidly (and quite violently) while shouting "Al can see ya!"

Kitchen entrance: alegre [a-LE-gre]. Alegre is an adjective that means happy. I see Allegra Geller, who is a character from a film called *eXistenZ* kissing Weird Al. This makes Weird Al very happy. If you know the film *eXistenZ* and the character Allegra Geller, then you know that this is a very strange and memorable image indeed.

Kitchen stove top: la alfomba [al-FOM-bra]. Alfombra means rug. For some reason, the image of Weird Al giving Alf an afro leaps to mind. Weird Al is also trying to unhook Alf's bar. Note: I'm getting into dangerous territory, because "fro" and "fom" are not at all the same. This is a perfect example of a word where I will need to go back and strengthen the image. However, for now I will carry on because speed of implementation is important with memory work. I can always come back and clean up later.

How to Learn and Memorize Spanish Vocabulary

Kitchen sink: algo [AL-go]. Algo is a masculine pronoun that means "something." Here Weird Al is pouring a bottle that says "something" down the sink. The liquid is corrosive and is melting the sink in a very surreal way. Al is saying: "there's SOMETHING wrong here."

Kitchen Counter: el algodón [al-go-DON]. Algodón is a masculine noun that means cotton. Here, I see Al grabbing a crime Don by his cotton shirt and shouting "Go Don!"

Fridge: alguien [AL-gyen]. Alguien is a pronoun that means "someone." I see Al smashing the fridge with a hammer, screaming: "Hello? Is Alguien home?" Note: this is another weak example. In this case, the phrase I am thinking of is usually stated "is anyone home," and that is quite different than someone in most contexts. I also haven't got a very good sense of how the word is to be pronounced from the images and am relying upon brute force to sunder it from my mind. This image will need to be revisited.

Rocking chair: algunas veces [al-GU-nas-BE-ses]. Algunas veces is an adverb that means "sometimes." In this image, Weird Al is in the rocking chair and flicking goo from his nostrils at the two flower vases on the bookshelf. To remember that "veces" is pronounced as a "b," the vases are filled with bees instead of flowers. It is fitting that Al is using the rocking chair, because this is something that I sat in only sometimes.

Television stand: la almohada [al-mo-A-da]. Almohada is a feminine noun that means pillow. In this image, Weir Al is using the television in a pillow fight with Scotty, who was

48

once a figure in a television commercial for "Scotty's tissues." The commercial always talked about how the tissues were as soft as a pillow.

How to Learn and Memorize Spanish Vocabulary

Chapter 6: Example Memory Palace for the Letter C

I'll never forget my friend Kirk's apartment on Chester Road. We spent a lot of time there watching movies, listening to music and talking about the books we liked and the ideas they gave us.

In this palace, I have again picked a specific kind of word to work on: Spanish words that start with the latters "car." Kirk's place is fitting because he loves cars and even has a Gran Torino tattooed on his arm. It's that Torino that will be linked to each and ever "car" word in the examples to follow.

As ever, I have charted my journey so that I don't cross my path, nor do I wind up getting trapped.

Dining room table: la cara [KA-ra]. Cara is a feminine noun that means face. Kirk used to date a girl named Cara, so I see him tattooing her face next to the Torino on his arm. I was lucky with this one because of knowing Kirk's romantic history, but as previously discussed, coincidences happen a lot and they are well worth capitalizing on.

Kitchen counter: la carne [KAR-ne]. Carne is another feminine noun, the word for meat. Here I see Kirk wearing a skirt while cutting up his own tattooed arm as if it were meat. To compound this, I am including that la carnicerí [kar-nee-se-REE-a], another feminine noun, is the word for butchery or meat market. To get the "seeeery" sound, I have Kirk cutting an entire series of his arm, as though he had duplicated them somehow.

Fridge: el carnicero [kar-nee-SE-ro]. This is a masculine noun that means butcher. Here I imagine Kirk putting his butchered arm in the fridge, which is now a prison. He's incarcerating it. He's also wearing boxing gloves, which makes the operation very awkward.

Kitchen entrance: caro [KA-ro] / cara [KA-ra]. This word is an adjective that changes gender depending on the word it modifies. It means "expensive." In this case, I see two Kirks standing in the doorway. One is carving an "oh" into his car tattoo, the other an "oh." In this image, the car has huge dollar signs instead of headlights.

Living room couch: la carretera [ka-rre-TE-ra]. Carretera is a feminine noun that means highway. In this image, Kirk's couch is painted like his tattoo on a highway and he is tearing the skirt it is wearing into pieces.

Television: la carta [KAR-ta]. This is a feminine noun which means "letter," as in the kind of letter you would mail to a friend. In this image, Kirk's car tattoo is now a mailbox eating a skirt-wearing shopping cart with postage stamps all over it.

Balcony entrance: el cartero [kar-TE-ro]. This is a masculine noun that means mail carrier.

Chapter 7: Example Memory Palace for the Letter E

I use my brother Eric's ski chalet in the mountains for the letter E. It's a very cozy place, and although I've only visited it a few times, I have no problem memorizing both the layout of the chalet, nor the surrounding area.

As always, I have started at the back of the palace and moved forward to prevent myself from getting trapped. I also make sure that I never cross my path in order to avoid confusing myself.

Finally, to speed my progress in learning, I pick a particular kind of E word, in the case of this example, "esc" words. I do this because it allows me to pick an image that can carry across a number of different stations. I like the idea of using the "esc" or escape key on a computer keyboard in combination with my brother.

This reminds me that all the words start with "esc." It gives me a human character to work with as well as an object. Not every image will have an escape key in it, so I first envision that my brother is wearing a T-shirt with an escape key on it to help compound the goal of this particular palace at this particular time.

Guest bedroom: la escalera [es-ka-LE-ra]. Escalera means staircase. In principle, this word is easy to remember because you can simply associate all staircases with a word you already know: escalator.

Nonetheless, we want to remember the gender. I see Eric building a staircase out of escape keys while wearing a skirt. The construction sign says "la escalera."

Guest bedroom entrance: el escáner [es-KA-ner]. Escáner is a masculine noun that means "scanner." Like la escalera, el escáner is nearly cognate with the English word, but to remember that it is masculine, I see my brother boxing with a scanner.

Main bedroom: la escoba [es-KO-ba]. La escoba, as signaled by "la," is a feminine noun that means "broom." In this image, I see my brother in a scuba suit, dying of oxygen deprivation because he is trying to inhale a tank filled with escape keys.

Bathroom: escoger [es-ko-JER]. Escoger is a verb that means to pick or to choose. Here I see my brother shoving escape keys into a jar marked "esco-JER." He is picking them up from the floor one by one in a very choosy way.

Hallway closet: esconder [es-kon-DER]. Esconder is a verb that means to hide. It is very similar to the English word "abscond," which means, essentially, to run away from or hide from the government in order to avoid punishment. Here I see my brother attempting to feed escape keys to a condor that is locked up in prison for attempting to hide. To strengthen the image, the condor is in the back of the cell trying to hide under a blanket.

Living room entrance: escribir [es-kree-BEER]. Escribir is a verb that means to write. Here I see my brother rocking a large crib. Inside is a crying infant in the shape of an escape key. This image is especially profound for me because my dad made a very beautiful crib for my brother and his family.

In front of the television: el escritorio [es-kree-TO-reeo]. Escritorio is a masculine noun that means "desk." Here I see my brother pounding a bunch of Oreo-cookie shaped escape keys on a desk. To compound the image, the same action is also playing on the television set.

Chapter 8: Choosing the Most Important Words

I've had many students approach me and say, "This is fantastic. I've been working at this and regularly memorize over a hundred words in a day. But what I don't really know is which words should I be focusing on in order to see the greatest improvement when it comes to fluency?"

This question is very good and very important. One of the first things a person can do is pop the phrase: "100 most important words in Spanish" into Google. You can also search for "Spanish word frequency." Doing this will give you plenty of lists from which to build a learning strategy.

In addition to those lists, I would like to share with you the words I have initially focused on in order to be able to understand as well as speak in the most intelligible ways as quickly as possible.

First, however, let me discuss a few points about learning and concentration. A more sophisticated understanding of these concepts will make for better Memory Palace experiences.

One way of thinking about learning and memorization is to see them as two different skills. However, learning a language is essentially memorizing its words so that you can use them with ease whenever you like. Fundamentally, then, all learning is memorization and all memorization is learning. The only question lurking in between, particularly with respect to language learning, is: do you have to understand what you've remembered in order to remember it.

The answer, of course, is a simple no. Many times I have learned a word and forgotten what it meant. As discussed in a previous chapter, this is why compounding images and rehearsal or revisiting the palaces frequently is so important.

However, there are some barriers that prevent us from taking these important steps. One of the biggest impediments is procrastination. We all procrastinate, and this is just something for the sake of sanity that we have to admit to ourselves. Since we all do it, there is really nothing to be gained from punishing ourselves or feeling bad about our procrastination. The fact of the matters is, that sitting around feeling bad for doing nothing inevitably leads to more sitting around doing nothing. It makes the problem worse.

The author Tim Ferris, who made his claim to fame with books such as *The 4 Hour Workweek* and *The Four Hour Body* discusses a very interesting method for dealing with procrastination. He allows it to happen. He knows it is inevitable, so he plans for it. One of the best quotes I've heard from him is that we should "budget for human nature instead of trying to conquer it."

Why am I telling you this? The reason is because in order to develop a substantial vocabulary in Spanish, you're going to need to spend some time. Although it really will take you only between 1-5 hours to build your full set of palaces, filling them with vocabulary is another matter.

When learning a second language, depending on your goals, you can literally spend a lifetime still developing your Memory Palaces. Despite my own achievements, when I sit down to read a sophisticated novel in Spanish, I need to put in some time extending my Memory Palaces and inserting new words.

But the point is that w mustn't punish ourselves for skipping a few days here and there. As Ferris suggests, we will do much better over the long haul if we routinely schedule the days we miss. Intentional procrastination can even be inspirational because as you are working, you know that some vegetation-time on the couch is just waiting for you to arrive and enjoy.

Four Ways to Choose the Words You Learn

The next issue is word selection. It is important to know what kinds of words you want to memorize, particularly in the beginning. There are four guidelines that you can use:

1. Examine the meaning of the words. This is a rather obvious point, but it is important because there are some words that you may not need to memorize right now. As well, it is important to pay attention to the grammatical function of the word. Verbs and adjectives may take more importance than nouns at particular times in your progression towards fluency. You might want to spend a month with each word type. By excluding word categories, you can actually learn a lot more, and also a lot more about the language itself and how it works.

2. Ask yourself: why is it that you want to know this particular word? Do you need the word for a particular meeting you're going to or to understand a book you're reading? Have you noticed it in the Spanish newspapers you've been glancing at? These are all important questions. You might also ask if the word is a synonym of other words you know. You should always be interested in learning synonyms. I recommend investing in a thesaurus (el tesauro). The reason why you should learn as many synonyms as you can is because you can add depth and flavor to your speaking. More importantly, if the person you are talking to doesn't quite understand why you are using a particular word, if you know some synonyms, you can essentially rotate them as if they were bullets in a gun, and eventually you will hit your target.
3. Consider how the word will be used in a sentence. If you cannot immediately think of how the word would be used, then search for an example using either an online dictionary or a print one that comes with complete sentence examples. It's always worth learning words even if you haven't got a feel for how to use them, but when working to overcome procrastination, you will feel that much more progress has been gained by learning words that you know you can put into practice with greater immediacy.
4. Inspire yourself by thinking about what you'll be able to achieve by having this new word firmly ensconced in your brain. This is a wonderful way to find motivation for learning. If you can imagine yourself being able to order a beer *and* compliment the waitress on her hairstyle, then you are essentially

using future pleasure to stimulate action in the now. And you will definitely feel very good when you notice how differently you are treated in comparison to other tourists who only learn the basics and leave it at that. People in other cultures genuinely love it when people not only learn their language, but use it on their own terms.

Here now is a list of the words I have discovered to be the most useful for fluency building. They are listed here alphabetically for easy placement into your own Memory Palace system.

Amount: el importe. This is the word you would use to discuss the check at a restaurant. If you wanted to talk about amounts in terms of quantity, then you would use the word la cantidad.

Argument: el argumento. Simple enough, but if you wanted to say "let's not argue about it," you would say "no discutamos." To say that something is beyond arguing, it is "indiscutible."

Beautiful: hermoso is common. However, you can also use bonita to talk about the beauty of a woman, bello to talk about the beauty of such things as scenery or poetry and precioso to discuss the beauty of a small animal or child. Belief: la creencia. But if something is hard to believe, you would use "incrédulo."

Certain: seguro or cierto. To be certain is seguro and to talk about a certain person would be "cierta persona."

Chance: casualidad, oportunidad or posibilidad. Notice that all of these words are a) near-cognates with the English terms and b) can all be associated with your father. With some imagination, you could create a palace reserved just for words that end with "dad."

Change: cambio. To say that something has changed for the better, you can say "un cambio a mejor." To say that it has changed for the worse, "un cambio a peor."

Clear: claro. A clear winner is "un claro vencedor." However, if you want to say that something is clear, you would say that your point is "evidente."

Common: también is used to say that you have something in common with someone. Something that is in commonly used, or frequently used is "frecuente."

Comparison: la comparación. But if you want to draw a comparison, you can say "establecer un paralelismo entre."

Condition: la condición. Knowing how to talk about the good or bad condition of something or someone is important. "En buen condiciones" is something in a good condition, whereas "mal estado condiciones" is used to talk about something in bad condition. If you want to say that you are going to do something, but only on one condition, then you would say "con una condición."

Connection: la conexión. It is important to note, however, that this word is used mostly for talking about connecting flights, trains or buses. "Relacionar" is more often used to show that there is a connection between two things, i.e. "bien relacionada" means to have a lot of social connections.

Decision: decisión. To say that you've made a decision, you can also use the word determinación.

Desire: la delectación. But if you want to talk about lust, the word is la lujuria. The desire or lust for power/money is la codicia.

Development: el desarrollo. But if you want to talk about development in terms of change, then use cambio, which we talked about under change.

Different: diferento or distinto. You can also use varios for various.

Education: la educación. If you want to talk about knowledge in general, la cultura is a better word.

Example: ejempio. This is a very important word. To say "for example," you would use, "por ejempio." You can turn this into a question by raising your voice at the end, much as you would in English. It is a great question to ask Spanish speakers often.

Existence: existencia. But to say that something is in existence, you would say existir. The opposite, which is to stop existing, is desaparecer.

Experience: la experiencia. If you want to say that you are

learning from your experience, remember that aprender means to learn. Therefore, you can say "aprendo de la experiencia."

Fact: el hecho. To say "in fact," simply say, de hecho.
Fear: el miedo or el temor. But "fear not," dear reader, and say: me temo que no.

Feeling: la sensibilidad. To have a feeling for something is "tener sensibilidad para algo." If you are talking about sentiment, you can use sentimiento.

Fiction: la ficción This is the word you would use to talk about a work of fiction, a.k.a. la literatura. To talk about fiction in the sense of something that has been invented, you can use invención.

Force: la fuerza can mean force in the sense of something you use, but it can also be used to talk about the police or the military as a noun.

Form: la forma. This is used to talk about everything from form and content (forma y contenido) or a form or madness (es una forma de locura).
Free: libre is used to express the condition of being free, whereas something is gratis or gratuito when it comes without incurring a financial charge.

Government: el gobierno. You'll find this one in the newspapers quite a bit. La politica gubernamental means "government policy."

History: la historia. If it happened in the past and belongs in the history books, you'll find it in a libro de historia.

Important: importante. It's important to be able to say that something is importante. It's equally important to be able to say "no tiene importancia" for it's not important.

Law: la ley. This is the word for both legal laws and physical laws, such as the law of gravity, which is called la ley de la graveded.

Mind: la mente. La mente literally means "thoughts." If you want to talk about your opinion, then the word is the same: opinión. To talk about changing your mind, you can use "cambiar de opinion." To be of the same mind is "ser de la misma opinion.

Motion: el movimiento. But to go through the motions is "cumplir con el formulismo de hacer algo."

Necessary: necesario. To do what is necessary is "hacer lo necesario." A necessary evil is "un mal necesario."

Observation: observación. You can also use comentario when you are making a remark about something.

Opposite: opuesto is the word to use when you mean the other side of the page, the street or the opposite short. To talk about the opposite sex, "el sexuo opuesto." Contrario is the word to use when you have an opposite opinion or want to go in the opposite direction. To talk about the house opposite to your own, you would say "la casa de enfrente."

How to Learn and Memorize Spanish Vocabulary

Pleasure: la satisfacción or el placer. You can also say "con mucho gusto" to say that you will do something with great pleasure.

Possible: possible. To be able to say "if possible" is very important. Use "si es posible."

Probably: problablemente.

Purpose: propósito. Objeto is also useful, particularly when you are talking about a specific aim.

Question: pregunta is the word when you are talking about questioning in the interrogative sense. A question mark is called "signo de interrogación. However, la duda is the word for doubt. To call something into question is therefore "poner algo en duda."

Reason: razón. You can also use motivo for motive. If something stands to reason, you would say that it is lógico or evidente.

Relation: pariente is the word to use in terms of a relative. Relación is the word to use when two things bear a connection.

Responsible: responsible.

Science: la ciencia. Science Fiction is Ciencia Ficción.

Simple: sencillo. To say it in simple terms would be

"sencillamente." But the simple truth is "la pura verdad."

Society: la sociedad. When someone is a danger to society, they are "un peligro para la socieded. If they belong to high culture, they are part of "la alta sociedad" Which group would you rather belong to?

Substance: la sustancia refers to matter. Substance abuse, on the other hand, is "abuso de narcóticos." If you want to talk about substance in terms of essences, use "esencia."

Thought: la idea or la reflexión. To give something a great deal of thought is to "relexionar mucho sobre algo."

True: cierto. But to say that something is factual, use the word "verdadero."

Unhappy: infeliz. You can also say that you are "no estar contento."

Way: camino. On the way is "en el camino." To go the wrong way is "equivocarse de camino."

There you have it. These words serve many purposes and you will encounter them often. If you use a dictionary to flesh out the definitions of these words, and better yet, a Spanish thesaurus, you will quickly find yourself in command of even more essential vocabulary. Words are very interconnected, and the more you learn, the more you can learn.

To really accelerate your learning, watch Spanish-language

movies, listen to Spanish-language music and read Spanish-language books, magazines and websites. Hearing and reading these words as they are used in real-time and in actual contexts is essential. Spending as little as 15-30 minutes a day on a regular basis will accelerate your learning experience greatly.

Finally, practice with intention. Break tasks down into components. By working on small parts with regularity and focus, you will achieve more than if you try to cram large parts into your brain in irregular blasts of attention. Build your palaces first, fill them with words and then rehearse.

Chapter 9: How to Use Relaxation for Vocabulary Memorization

A friend of mine suggested that I call this chapter "Relax to Rememberize," but I thought it rather too cute.

"Remembercize" was another suggestions – and I ultimately cannot disagree with the connotation that remembering is a kind of exercise.

Harry Lorayne has pointed out that one of the reasons why we can't remember the names of people we meet is because we haven't paid attention to them in the first place. I believe that tension, stress and not being present gets in the way of the attention needed for Memory Palace work.

The number one reason you want to be relaxed when you learn vocabulary is because it will *train you to be relaxed when you are trying to recall the words in normal conversation*. Nothing is worse than knowing a word, but being unable to recall it due to nervousness or feeling like you are on the spot.

To that end, I want to share with you some principles of breathing that you can use while memorizing vocabulary. Since so many of us experience confidence issues around our memories, we need relaxation in order to overcome such boundaries. Fortunately, this is easily done.

The two main strategies I use have wider applications than memory work alone. I recommend using them every day for general health as well.

I know of nine breathing techniques overall, one of which I will discuss in this chapter. It is called Pendulum breathing. The second involves progressive muscle relaxation.

Pendulum Breathing

If you've ever seen a pendulum, then you know that there is an interesting moment at the end of each cycle where the pendulum seems to hang for an instant and then move a little bit more in the first direction before falling back the other way. It does this back and forth. Pendulum Breathing works much in this way.

To start with Pendulum breathing, fill your lungs normally, and then pause slightly. Instead of exhaling, breathe in a little bit more. Let the breath out naturally and pause. Instead of inhaling, exhale out a little bit more. By circulating your breath in this way, you are "swinging" the air like a pendulum. This practice will reduce stress in your overall life once you are used to doing it, but if you do nothing else, implement pendulum breathing in your memory work. This method of breathing makes Memory Palace construction and the generation of images and associations so much easier because you are putting yourself in a kind of oxygenated dream state.

At first, it may seem difficult to concentrate on both your breathing and doing imaginative Memory Palace building.

In some ways, it is like being a drummer who is creating three or four different patterns, one for each limb. With practice, the ability will come to you. The best part is that this form of practice is incredibly relaxing.

Progressive Muscle Relaxation

Progressive Muscle Relaxation is relatively well-known, and yet so few people practice it. The work is simple: sit on a chair or lie down on a bed or the floor. Next:

1) Point your toes upward and hold.
2) Point your toes towards the wall and hold.
3) Flex your calves.
4) Flex your thighs.
5) Flex your buttocks.
6) Flex your stomach muscles, lower back muscles, chest and shoulders (all core muscles).
7) Flex your hands, forearms and upper arms.
8) Flex your neck, your cheeks and the muscles surrounding your eyes.

Practice Pendulum Breathing as you do this, or at least work to conjoin the flexing movements with your breathing.

Once you have achieved a profound state of relaxation and all of your 27 memory palaces have been built, sit with a dictionary or a list of the specific words you wish to remember and their meanings. If isolating the terms helps you, prepare an index card for each word.

As mentioned in a previous chapter, I recommend that you

keep an Excel file for the purposes of testing. To do this, without looking at your list, you will write down all of the words you have memorized and only then compare them against the original list.

Otherwise, avoid rote learning at all costs. Let your Memory Palace skills do the work. Compound your images when testing routines reveal weaknesses. Just as you would relax to remember, relax to test and relax to compound as well. Again, realize that you want to practice relaxation during memorization so that you condition yourself to be relaxed when accessing the words later during conversations with others.

Conclusion

Next time you are out for a walk, shopping or just wandering around the house, consider the hundreds of locations you can use to build and extend your Memory Palaces. The more you pay attention to your surroundings, the more material you will have to work with. As well, take every opportunity to visit places you've previously lived or gone to school. Revitalizing your familiarity with the locations you use to build your Memory Palaces is not entirely necessary, but at the very least, you should perform a mental walkthrough to ensure that you have enough material for at least the first 10 stations and ideally many more.

In addition, utilize the power of your imagination and the images it brings you. Harness the power of coincidences such as those I related in the example palaces. Use the principles discussed in this book and suit them to your own needs. Never be afraid to play around, amplify and use absurdities. Test yourself and compound. And always, always relax when doing memory work.

Spend time thinking about the kinds of words you would like to learn or need to know. Analyze how you can group different word forms together and develop your vocabulary based on the form of the language. You will see many more connections by doing this.

Speak as often as you can. Hold what an associate of mine named Joshua Smith calls "natural conversations" in a book he wrote for ESL students called "Breaking Through to Fluency." This means taking the simple conversational patterns you learn on the recorded Spanish trainings out into the real world and seeing how they are really used by real people. If you live in North America, there are countless ways to meet with Spanish speakers and engage with them. Meetup.com is now available in countless cities and Craigslist is a good resource. If you cannot find possibilities online, ask at your local library. They will certainly know about your local Spanish-speaking community and point you in the right direction.

Finally, teach others what you have learned about memorization skills. Tell them how you built your Memory Palaces, the techniques of imagery and activity and give them some examples of how you've memorized specific words. Teaching is one of the best ways to compound what you've learned and to see other possibilities you may have missed.

I wish you a lot of fun with these techniques and great progress with your Spanish language endeavors. I would be pleased if you contacted me to let me know how you've done, and if this book has helped you, please leave a review on Amazon so that others can learn this skill too. Remember: the more you learn, the more you *can* learn. The same is true with memory. The more you remember, the more you have learned. And learning a new language is a special achievement indeed.

About the Author

Anthony Metivier completed his BA and MA in English Literature at York University in Toronto, Canada. He earned a second MA in Media and Communications from The European Graduate School in Switzerland while completing a PhD in Humanities, also from York. As the author of scholarly articles, fiction and poetry, he has taught Film Studies in Canada, the United States and Germany. He plays the electric bass.

More Memorization Resources

In this section I will describe to you how that I have modified the larger principles described in the previous chapter to my own purposes as part of reaching my goal of easily memorizing the Spanish language.

In other words, in this chapter and the next, I'll tell you how I raised the seat, adjusted the handlebars and polished the chrome in order to be sure the bicycle of memory techniques suited my needs perfectly. I will also discuss four ways that I use memory on a daily basis and give you examples of each.

Although you may not use your memory to retain poetry, the order of a deck of cards or the number of your car and seat on a train in Spain, my hope is that you'll follow my descriptions of how I put these larger principles into action and see how to apply them in your own way.

Please don't skip this section. There are many important clues and ideas that you can use on your own journey towards memorizing Spanish vocabulary. These exercises were essential to me and they will be essential to you.

Poetry and Novels

I know that we're not here to learn memory tricks, but there is little that impresses people more than the ability to whip out a heap of Shakespeare off the top of your head. I'm not talking about "To be or not to be." I'm talking about the entire soliloquy.

Poetry can be difficult to remember, especially if it is unrhymed or has an unusual rhyme structure. Take John Keats's *Ode to a Nightingale*, for example. I love the second stanza:

> O for a draught of vintage! That hath been
> Cool'd a long age in the deep-delved earth
> Tasting of Flora and the country green.
> Dance, Provencal song, and sunburnt mirth!
> O for a beaker full of the warm South!
> Full of the true, the blushing Hippocrene
> With beaded bubbles winking at the brim
> And purple-stained mouth
> That I might drink and leave the world unseen
> And with thee fade away into the forest dim

Good stuff, no?

Now, how did I memorize it? Well, as discussed in the previous chapter I started by picking a location. As it happens, I had first encountered this poem in a classroom in Winters College at York University where I took some of my four degrees.

I remember the room where I studied the poem and the entire building very well. So that's where I started.

Remember: we use places that we know precisely because we don't have to remember them. If I know where the door is in relation to the desk where I sat, then there is no need to remember that the desk is station one and the door is station too. It just happens naturally.

So let's begin. Here is how I memorized this delightful, if sad stanza from one of Keats' most heartfelt poems.

O for a draught of vintage!

I imagined myself as large and as vibrantly as possible squeezed into the tiny desk I sat in when class was in session. I saw myself drawing the word "vintage" using dark black pencil. The pencil is enormous and digs deeply into the surface of the desk like a knife. To get more action into the scene, I imagined myself working feverishly, like a mad draftsman trying to express some unspeakable secret.

That hath been
Cool'd a long age in the deep-delved earth

By the door leading out of the classroom, I pictured a fridge, and there I saw myself digging earth out of it with a shovel. I stabbed the earth deeply with the shovel and tossed the dirt into the hall.

Tasting of Flora and the country green.

Outside in the hall, I saw myself painting the concrete wall with flowers and a green countryside. This time I was a mad painter and this time, to remember the line, I visualized myself tasting the paint.

How to Learn and Memorize Spanish Vocabulary

Dance, Provencal song, and sunburnt mirth!

By the door of the next classroom down the hall, I saw myself dancing, and then kicking Ezra Pound through the bars of a prison. For reasons I won't get into, Pound is readily associated with Provencal songs by people who majored in English. Pound also went through a period in his life where he was caged beneath the sun, and according to legend he laughed at the guards a lot. So I saw him laughing at me as I kicked him, his face badly burnt by the sun.

O for a beaker full of the warm South!

For this line I had to bent the rules of reality. There is a third classroom in Winters College on that floor, and I simply imagined that it was a scientific laboratory. Inside, I imagined a mad scientist violently cracking an egg-shaped compass pointing south into a bubbling beaker. The smoke and boiling bubbles helped me remember that the South Keats speaks of is warm.

Full of the true, the blushing Hippocrene

For this image, I moved into the staircase at the end of the corridor. I imagined a blushing Hippopotamus with his mouth full of college degrees, his belly stuffed to the brim with them.

With beaded bubbles winking at the brim

This one was easy. In the basement of Winters College is a pub run for and by students. I just saw myself trying to bead the brim of a wine glass with a needle and some thread. And of course, everything was huge, vibrant and visualized with over-the-top action. For example, I wasn't just "trying" to push a needle into the glass, but stabbing at it frantically. The imagery is kind of disturbing, but that's exactly the point. That's what makes it memorable.

That I might drink and leave the world unseen

Brace yourself for more grotesque violence. To remember this, I saw myself drinking from the glass and then stabbing myself in the eyes with the needle.

And with thee fade away into the forest dim

The patio outside the pub isn't exactly like a forest, but I still used it. I populated it with trees, made it dark, and envisioned myself being guided into the forest as the entire picture dimmed out, like the ending of a film.

In truth, memorizing the passage was not a great deal of work, partly because I love the poetry. Being able to pay attention to the subtleties of the language and Keats' particular spin on the world not only helps, but creates a sense of urgency for me. I not only want to know Keats better, but I *need* to know his poetry better. This is what I tell myself. I manufacture excitement when I don't feel it naturally.

Paradoxically, I combine this sense of excitement with deep relaxation when working. This combination of excitement and relaxation helps came easily to me because I just relaxed and let them come to me. In about half an hour, I was able to recite the passage with ease.

When it comes to novels, the procedure is more or less the same. But instead of memorizing individual lines, I remember important plot points and the names of characters. Character names don't necessarily have to be remembered because the novelist will use them over and over again and in many cases we'll come to identify with the characters and remember their names naturally and without any external effort.

It helps too if you understand the shapes novels tend to take. Usually there is some kind of problem or dilemma experienced by a character who is faced by something that has happened in his or her past. The dilemma then turns into a crisis that must be dealt with, followed by a strong decision and a series of actions leading to a battle or confrontation with the antagonist. There may be a moment of self-revelation during the battle that helps the character defeat the antagonist, followed by the resolution. Obviously, not every story has this exact shape, but thinking in terms of story shape can certainly help as you work on memorizing the elements of the plot.

The important thing to keep in mind is the kind of space you use. If you are memorizing 8-10 lines of poetry, then it's possible that a single room or a small apartment with several rooms will do. I usually prefer to use one room or location for this kind of work, but if you are able to compress things in your memory palace, you could imagine a bookshelf in a room you are familiar with and use each individual book as either a portal to another memory palace or as an individual signifier of what you want to remember. It's all up to you.

But when it comes to remembering the key events of a novel, make sure that you have a big enough place so that you don't run out of stations. I wouldn't want to use Winters College to remember Tolstoy's *War and Peace*, for instance, but for something like that, Broadway in Manhattan would probably do. It's a long walk from 187 where I used to live down to the southern most tip of Broadway, but I've done it, the streets are numbered and you can easily follow it in a sequence that's hard to miss.

If you are a film reviewer, or just want to memorize the plot points of the films you see, it may take some practice to get fast enough to create vibrant, memorable and active images and store them in unique locations in real-time, but it can be done. You can also take notes and then memorize these later when you can relax.

On that note, I must say it again: one of the key points in all of memory practice that no other memory book I've read mentions is that you need to make sure that you are relaxed. If you are feeling tense or running away from a mugger (which you might be on the stretch of Broadway that runs through Manhattan), these techniques probably won't have the desired effect.

I mention this mugging example for a reason. I was once the victim of an attempting mugging on Broadway in Harlem. I know the area quite well, but I cannot use it as part of any Memory Palace because of that experience. My heart always quickens when I think of that gun pointed at me. This touch of anxiety interferes with the memorization process immensely. Keep this point in mind when building your memory palaces.

Here are some action steps that you can take immediately to start practicing the memorization of poetry:

1) Pick a poem you actually enjoy. Although it is certainly possible to memorize material you could care less about, obviously for the purposes of practice, you want to enjoy "owning" the material in your head.

2) As always, make sure that you plan out in advance where you are going to store the material. Make sure that you are familiar with the locations and that you've "cleaned" them out. If you've used the location before, you might run into some trouble if memories from the past are still lurking there.

3) Work on your memory only when you are relaxed.

4) Avoid falling back on rote memory attempts. They can sneak up so easily, but are not the point of the exercise. Use the techniques of location, imagery and action.

5) Test yourself, but in a way that doesn't involve rote learning. If you make a mistake, go back and examine the imagery you've chosen. Is it strong enough? What might you need to add in order to make it stronger?

6) Talk to someone about the efforts you are making. This is one of the best ways to solidify your results. If you can, teach them how to do what you are doing. Teaching is not only personally edifying, but it helps to make the world a better place. And remember, the more you can remember, the more you can remember.

7) Avoid using places where stressful memories might interfere with the memorization process.

Memorize a Deck of Cards

Warning: The exercises in this next section may seem unusual. Yet, I've included them because I feel that all of this information is essential to your travels on the path to memorizing Spanish vocabulary.

What could be so unusual, you ask? Imagine the following scenario.

You're seated with some friends in a restaurant. You have 52 individual objects on the table. They're quite small and easily stored in your pocket. These objects can be assembled and reassembled at will. Each object has a unique set of images on the front and look virtually identical on the back. In fact, you have to turn each one over to spot the difference between one object and another.

You have the objects out on the table because your friends have been asking you exactly how you've come to have such a powerful memory. Because you know that one of the best ways to master something is to teach it to someone else, you've decided to teach them the skills you learned in this book.

But first you want to give them a demonstration.

Imagine that you ask one of your friends to reorder the objects. They can spend as much time as they like.
Once they're done, they hand the objects to you. You turn them over one at a time, look at the fronts and then turn them back over, hiding their unique features from your line of sight for the rest of the demonstration.

When you've gotten through all 52 objects, you have the objects back to your friend. To create a bit of time delay, you recite the alphabet backwards or a new poem you've recently created.

Then, you ask your friend to look at the front of the first object.

You tell him what it is.

Your proceed to the next object and then the next and the next until you've correctly named all 52.

Your friends are amazing. You feel wonderful. You are now in a position to teach.

What are these 52 unique objects you've remembered with such tremendous ease?

Yes, you've guessed it: a deck of cards.

Would you like to be able to do what I've just described? Then read on, because the techniques in this chapter involve memorizing a deck of cards. More importantly, this skills is an important step towards finessing your brain for the memorization of Spanish vocabulary.

Admittedly, effectively memorizing a deck of cards is quite complex, at least to get started. However, do the groundwork and you'll find many more applications for the raw tools you'll need to cultivate that are applicable in numerous ways, learning Spanish being just one of them. If nothing else, setting yourself up to be able to memorize a deck of cards quickly and efficiently will give you great exercise in the discipline needed in the Preparation and Determination department.

Think about this skill in terms of the Karate Kid.

Remember the way Mister Miyagi made young Daniel-san wash cars and mop the floor. There seemed to be no purpose in it, certainly not in terms of reaching his goals with karate. Yet, when the time came to actually implement karate skills, blammo, Daniel-san had them all at hand. So please don't underestimate the power of squats and pushups, which is essentially what this chapter is all about.

All that said, let me note that I also wanted to learn how to memorize the order of a randomly shuffled deck for the purposes of doing amazing magic tricks. I wound up gaining a lot more in the process, about memory, about the Spanish language and about myself. Ultimately, there's no direct way to describe how and why this process helped me with the acquisition of Spanish other than to say that I couldn't have figured out the path without taking each and every step of my particular journey.

I also learned a lot about what doesn't work for me when it comes to memorizing things during this stage of my memory journey. That is why I am sharing these details with you.

And so: following the technical description of how I learned to memorize a deck of cards, I'll follow up with the example of how I use this system to memorize the seat number on my train, or anything else I might want to remember that this system can help with.

There are a number of stages in being able to memorize a deck of randomized cards quickly and effectively.

First, we need to learn a method of organizing the cards. We do this by giving each card a number. Since there are 52 cards in the deck, we need to divide them up according to suite and then give each suite a number. I'll explain the rationale behind these numbers in a moment, but for now, let's say that:

>Spade = 10
>Diamonds = 30
>Clubs = 50
>Hearts = 80

Now let me explain why we have designated these suites

with these numbers. It has to do with a numerical sound system that works like this (believe it or not, remembering this simple list of sounds is really the hardest part of the job – the rest is just a technical application of the list):

> 1 = ta/da
> 2 = na
> 3 = ma
> 4 = ra
> 5 = la
> 6 = cha/ja
> 7 = ka
> 8 = fa/va
> 9 = ba/pa
> 0 = sa

I know what you must be thinking: these memory people are nuts! Well, there is some truth to that, but let's carry on with developing the technique.

Remember that we said the Spades are assigned the number 10. The reason for this will start to become clear when you look at the following:

> Ace of Spades = 11 (Toad)
> 2 of Spades = 12 (Tin)
> 3 of Spades = 13 (Dam)
> 4 of Spades = 14 (Tire)
> 5 of Spades = 15 (Tail)
> 6 of Spades = 16 (Dish)
> 7 of Spades = 17 (Tack)
> 8 of Spades = 18 (TV)

9 of Spades = 19 (Tape)
10 of Spades = 20 (Nose)
Jack of Spades = 21 (Nut)
Queen of Spades = 22 (Nun)
King of Spades = 23 (Enemy)

Now, we start with the Ace of Spades as the number 11 simply to give the order a nicer sequence. Since the sound for 1 is "ta" or "da," I have made the word Toad as my association for the Ace of Spades. You could come up with whatever word you like based on "ta" or "da" sounds, but I would recommend that you pick something that can be easily imagined and placed into action in some way.

Just to be clear how the sequence works, I'll point out that the 2 of Spades is "Tin" in my system because the sound for 1 is "ta" (or "da") and the sound for 2 is "na." Therefore, 12, which is the 2 of Spades could be "tan," or "dan." Surely there are other options, but "tin" has always worked well for me.

Another tip that you might find useful is to pick words that have some personal meaning if you can. 3 of Spades is "dam" for me, not only because as a card associated with 13 is "dam" a logical word, but it also reminds me of when my father worked on a huge dam-building project. He brought me out there a few times, and to my childlike imagination, it was amazing to see the scope of that project. In fact, I think it would probably seem pretty amazing to anyone of any age. The point here is that the more personal the image is, the more staying power it has.

Now, assuming you have this system in place, let me briefly explain why after the 9 of Spades, we switch from words that start with "t" or "d" to words that start with "n." The reason is that the 9 is represented as the 19th card in the sequence, and since 1 is "ta" and 9 is "pa," I have chosen the word "tape." The Jack of Spades, however, is the 20th card. Since 2 is a "na" sound and 0 is a "sa" sound, I have selected the word "nose."

Before I give you my personal keywords for the rest of the deck, let me give you a quick example of how I would use this system just using a single suite. Let's say that I want to remember that the 9 of Spades comes on top of the 3 of Spades in a stack I am trying to memorize. I would imagine a giant role of tape manically wrapping up a huge concrete dam.

Later, when I wanted to remember which order the two cards came in, it would simply be a matter of remembering the absurd image of a roll of tape crazily unraveling over the surface of a dam, as if to secure it from cracking apart in an earthquake. In fact, in order to really make it memorable, I might want to add a detail like that. This is called "giving the association a reason." If there is a reason, no matter how absurd, that a role of tape is wrapping up a large concrete structure, then it can help with remembering it.

Let's carry on to see how I've portioned out the Diamonds using this system. Since the Diamonds fall under the number 30, most of this suite will start with "m" words. But as in every suite, we eventually come to the next group of 10, which means that the 10 of diamonds will start with an 'r' word.

    Ace of Diamonds = 31 (Maid)
    2 of Diamonds = 32 (Man)
    3 of Diamonds = 33 (Mime)
    4 of Diamonds = 34 (Mare)
    5 of Diamonds = 35 (Mail)
    6 of Diamonds = 36 (Match)
    7 of Diamonds = 37 (Muck)
    8 of Diamonds = 38 (Movie)
    9 of Diamonds = 39 (Map)
    10 of Diamonds = 40 (Rice)
    Jack of Diamonds = 41 (Rat)
    Queen of Diamonds = 42 (Ran)
    King of Diamonds = 43 (Ram)

Clubs:

    Ace of Clubs = 51 (Lad)
    2 of Clubs = 52 (Lion)
    3 of Clubs = 53 (Lamb)
    4 of Clubs = 54 (Lyre)
    5 of Clubs = 55 (Lily)
    6 of Clubs = 56 (Leash)
    7 of Clubs = 57 (Lock)
    8 of Clubs = 58 (Leaf)
    9 of Clubs = 59 (Leap)
    10 of Clubs = 60 (Cheese)
    Jack of Clubs = 61 (Cheetah)
    Queen of Clubs = 62 (Chain)
    King of Clubs = 63 (Gym)

And finally:

    Ace of Hearts = 81 (Fat)

2 of Hearts = 82 (Fan)
3 of Hearts = 83 (Foam)
4 of Hearts = 84 (Fire)
5 of Hearts = 85 (Foil)
6 of Hearts = 86 (Fish)
7 of Hearts = 87 (Fake)
8 of Hearts = 88 (Fife)
9 of Hearts = 89 (Viper)
10 of Hearts = 90 (Bus)
Jack of Hearts = 91 (Boat)
Queen of Hearts = 92 (Bone)
King of Hearts = 93 (Bomb)

These are the words I've come up with for each card using the numerical-sound system, but it's up to you to pick the words and images that work best for you.

Now, let me tell you how I put all of this together. Do you remember how I said that I sometimes have portals inside of my memory palaces that lead to unusual places? My memorized deck of cards is an example of this.

I have lived in two apartments in the capital of Germany, Berlin. I really liked my office in the first apartment and have used it a lot to memorize many things. In the mental version of that office as I have remembered it, there is a pack of red Bicycle playing cards (I just realized now that it may be from the cards that I got the idea of explaining to people that memory systems are just like bikes!)

But instead of playing cards inside that box, there is a garage. If you've seen Christopher Nolan's second Batman film, *The Dark Knight*, you'll know the kind of space I'm talking about. In that film, Batman's "Batcave" is actually a sophisticated room, open and bright with plenty of room for automobiles.

But I don't have any fancy sports cars or Batmobiles in my garage (inside a card box in an office in an apartment in Berlin). Instead, I have the first four cars I owned as a teenager. I have the cars lined up in order from the first car to the fourth car (which also happened to be the last car I ever owned before turning to transit and rental cars only).

The first car is my blue Volkswagen Beetle. It was lowered to the ground and very special to me. Too bad I wrecked it. My second car was an orange Volkswagen Beetle. There was nothing particularly special about it, but I miss it even to this day.

My third car was a silver Ford Fiesta. A bizarre choice, but I loved it.

My fourth car was a blue Chevy Malibu.

For the purposes of this Memory Palace, each car has 13 locations, which works nicely because each suite in a deck also has 13 cards.

The locations I use are:

> The front driver's side headlight
> The front passenger's side headlight
> The engine hood

The windshield
The steering wheel
The driver seat
The passenger seat
The seat behind the driver's seat
The seat behind the passenger's seat
The inside of rear window
The outside of the rear window
The trunk
The exhaust pipe

For some people, these stations might be too closely compressed together, but this arrangement works very well for me. In general, I like my stations to be as close together as possible.

The nice thing about each car having 13 locations is that I don't feel like I have to memorize an entire deck. Instead, I only need to remember 13 cards per car. It's ultimately rather arbitrary, but it still has a psychological effect that helps the task seem less daunting.
So, taking thirteen cards, let's see what the first car might look like:

Front driver's side headlight = 3 of Clubs (Lamb)
Front passenger's side headlight = 8 of Hearts (Fife)
Engine Hood = 7 of Spades (Tack)
Windshield = 6 of Spades (Dish)
The steering wheel = 10 of Spades (Nose)
The driver seat = Ace of Clubs (Lad)

How to Learn and Memorize Spanish Vocabulary

        The passenger seat = Ace of Diamonds (Maid)
        The seat behind the driver's seat = Jack of Spade (Nut)
        The seat behind the passenger's seat = 3 of Diamonds (Mime)
        The inside of rear window = 9 of Clubs (Leap)
        The outside of the rear window = 10 of Diamonds (Cheese)
        The trunk = 5 of Spades (Tail)
        The exhaust pipe – 5 of Clubs (Lily)

Now it's just a matter of using location, imagery and activity to weave these images together. It's actually very easy and fun.

Just imagine a lamb standing in front of the car with a fife in his mouth. In addition to the horrible music the lamb is blaring from where he is not standing in front of the passenger side headlight, tacks are firing rapidly over the hood from the fife and smashing into the dish hovering over the windshield. Pieces of shrapnel from the dish have smashed into the nose on the steering wheel, which belongs to the lad sitting in the driver's seat. He winds up sneezing all over the maid sitting in the passenger's seat and so she steals a handkerchief from Nutty Jack of Spades in the back seat who is hitting on the mime beside him. She tries to leap through the window, but crashes her head against a huge chunk of cheese and just as she is recovering, she finds herself being smashed in the face by the tail of the dog I hate, Lily.

It seems like a lot of work, and it is. But with practice, it gets faster and easier. You'll even begin to find that you don't really need all the "training wheels" I've described as much as you did in the beginning, though they will still always be there to help you and will always remain the basic foundation of how you remember the cards. The best part is that you'll find your concentration sharpening and your attention for detail widening. It's a great mental exercise that you won't regret taking up as a habit.

Plus, it will serve as an excellent part of your goal of being able to effortlessly remember Spanish so that you can learn the language quickly and efficiently.

A few notes on this chapter:

I do not use "ran" as a verb for the Queen of Diamonds. Here I am thinking of the Kurosawa movie *Ran*, which is a samurai adaptation of Shakespeare's *King Lear*. I actually don't picture a woman here, but the old man as he is seen sitting in ceremonial dress at the beginning of the movie. Lily, the 5 of Clubs is not a flower, but a dog a friend of mine used to have as a pet. I never liked that dog very much, which makes it all the more effective as a memory prompt, ironically.

Leap for the 9 of Clubs is the one spot where I use a verb. I would rather not have, but I couldn't find any other image that worked for me. "Lap" would be a natural choice, but since laps don't actually exist, at least not once a person is standing, this image just doesn't work for me.

As a final note to this chapter, I want to tell you a little about what didn't work for me when it came to memorizing a deck of cards. The great magician Juan Tamirez gives a number of strategies.

One method is to sing the order of the deck as you want to learn it. Record yourself singing the order and listen to the recording again and again. This approach is perfectly fine, so long as you want to remember a pre-arranged deck that is always pre-arranged in the memorized order. Sometimes, this is my preference, since I am adept at appearing to shuffle a deck without disturbing the order of the cards. Nonetheless, singing the order never worked for me. It amounts to learning by rote.

Another idea Tamirez gives is to arbitrarily assign both a number and an animal to each and every card. This is getting closer to the system I ultimately landed upon, but it still leads one to use rote memorization in place of a system that lets you remember the order of the cards almost instantly. Now that I've shared with you both what has worked for me and what hasn't, let me suggest a few …

Action steps:

1) Make the commitment to memorize the sound system for the ten digits, 0 – 9. It's very easy.

2) Apply the number sounds to the different suits in the manner described.

3) Make a word for each card using the number system. Using a written list, Word file or Excel sheet, store the

words you create so that you can test your memory of them later.

4) Decide in advance where you are going to store the order of the cards you will be memorizing. Use actual locations or invent them. Since you need 52 for this exercise, it is best to think of how you can compress them into a smaller space.

5) Make sure that you are relaxed throughout this process. Training yourself to be relaxed while working on memory techniques helps with recall. You want to "anchor" the sensation of relaxation so that you know it very well. You'll instantly fall into that state of relaxation at any time you want to with dedicated practice.

6) Get out a deck of cards, shuffle it, and begin memorizing it.

7) Test everything, but always make sure that you are not falling back on rote memory. That is not the purpose of these exercises.

8) Describe to someone else the procedures that you are using. You do not need to show off. Simply explain what you are doing and your progress with it. Give a demonstration if you like, but focus on teaching the method whenever possible. Doing so will enhance your skills. Always make sure to demystify these

memory techniques as difficult or something to be reserved for nerds or geniuses or people who are otherwise weird. Memory skills are for everyone.

Spread the word!

Do you like this book? Has it helped you to memorize Spanish vocabulary with tangible results? If so, I want to ask you to help me tell other people about it.

Since 2007 I've made my living entirely by writing and teaching. Yet, I have done very little promotion for my books (though this is currently changing). Nearly every sale has come from people passing on the good news through word of mouth. So now I'm asking YOU to please help me spread the word.

Here's how you can help.

If you have an email list of friends and contacts, why not send them a message about this book and its contents?

Discuss the book on web forums and message boards.

Print out a few relevant pages and leave them in any common area where you work or meet with people. You can print your name on the copies so that people know they belong to you and use the material to start great conversations about memorization.

If you have friends or contacts in the press or media, tell them about this book. They will definitely get a good story, article or feature out of it. I can easily be contacted by emailing: rhizomatic@zoho.com.

Write a review of the book and tell people where they can

find it.

If you write guest blogs or speak on podcasts, mention how this book has helped you.

Do you teach Spanish as a second language or memorization skills? Maybe this book can be included as part of your course or your next product launch. You could also invite me to be a speaker and have me offer your students individualized coaching while I'm there. Contact me for details.

Thank you.

Anthony Metivier
rhizomatic@zoho.com

SECRET BONUS SECTION

To thank you for reading this book, I want to give you a special bonus. Think of this section as one of those hidden tracks some artists put at the end of their CDs.

When I teach memory skills in a live setting, I haven't got a whole lot of time to impress my students while I'm teaching them the memory techniques discussed in this book. Let's face it: we used to live in an instant on world. Now it's a world of instant downloads. People want the skills I have to offer and they want them immediately.

Here's what I've come up with to create that effect. Within fifteen minutes, I teach them to recite the entire alphabet backwards. It's strange that we cannot do this naturally and equally strange that we need to go to such elaborate lengths in order to train ourselves to do it, but it's worth the effort. Saying the alphabet backwards is the equivalent of skipping rope with your brain. It sends oxygen rich blood to your brain and will wake you up any time you need a kickstarter. And it's healthier than coffee!

Having read this book, you already have the basis for how to do accomplish this feat. There's actually two ways to do it.

Option One: Create a 26 station Memory Palace. Place 26 objects, one per station. The only rule is that each object must start with a letter of the alphabet in reverse order, i.e. zebra, yolk, xylophone, weathervain, etc. As with all memory techniques, the process works best if you create your own words.

Option Two: Create a highly memorable story. This method uses a linking system taught in this book. I didn't teach it because with the exception of using it to memorize the alphabet backwards, I personally don't use it. For more on the linking technique, I recommend reading any of the books mentioned in the resources section.

Here's the story that I use to memorize the alphabet backwards:

Zebras with **Y**ellow **X**ylophones ask **W**hat to a German man named **VUT** who is a **SR** (Senior) with a **Q**uestion for the **P**ost **O**ffice in **N**orthern **M**innesota, **L**ake **K**ilimanjaro where **J**esus asks **I** (me) about the **H**uman **G**rowth **F**ormula created by the **E**ducation **D**epartment of the **C**entral **B**rain **A**dministration.

I use Option One in class to teach my students how to say the alphabet backwards, but I do it in a sneaky way. I *never* tell them that the goal is to say the alphabet backwards. I simply have them first draw a memory palace for themselves with 10 stations. I give them ten words. When they are sufficiently impressed with their ability to recall the first ten words (zebra, yolk, xylophone, etc), I have them repeat the process with a second memory palace.

With another ten words down the hatch and everyone reciting all twenty words with ease, I ask one of the students to recite the words again, but this time saying only the first letter of each word. It rarely dawns on the person speaking what they are achieving, but within seconds, the rest of the class is stunned.

Five minutes later, the students have added six more words and everyone is reciting the alphabet backwards with ease. Try this for yourself. You'll love it!

Introducing Magnetic Memory Coaching on Skype!

This program is YOUR chance to receive personalized training in:

- Powerful Memory Techniques
- Effective Time-Management Strategies for Fitting It All In
- Recall Practice and Mastery That Will Ensure That You Never Accidentally Fall Back on Rote Learning
- Guided Memory Palace Construction for People Struggling to Tap the Potential of Their Imaginations
- … and other skills, ideas and personal traits that are so important to your success with Magnetic Memorization.

This program of individualized coaching in a **one-to-one** setting on Skype or by telephone runs from September-December, January-April and June-August.

To help you learn the elegant skills and strategies of Magnetic Memory, I design our sessions to:

- Walk you through *how* and *why* each technique works
- Tell you *exactly what to do* through each step
- Show you how to modify the techniques for your own needs
- Give you exercises to reinforce the skills and acquire new vocabulary or memorize anything you want

Reality Check

Before signing up for coaching, you should know that in order for the techniques you'll learn with me to work, I'll need you to implement them. This is, after all, what coaching is for! In full disclosure, I must tell you that although all of these strategies have worked miracles for me personally and all of my students, there is no such thing as a magic bullet. But if you practice what you'll learn with me, I guarantee that you'll be very glad that you made this investment in your development. In fact, I guarantee that you'll be *unbeatable* when it comes to memorizing whatever you want.

What They Say

"Dr. Metivier's brilliant intellectual style and teaching philosophy warrants special attention. He helped me develop my memory as a key tool for my life."

Nils Peiler

"Anthony is possessed of one of the most impressive minds you are likely ever to encounter. He is one of those rare individuals who simply "gets it" when it comes to helping people improve their memory – and he is possessed of that rare enthusiasm common to all great teachers."

Brennan Mitchell

"Without exaggerating, the time I spent with Dr. Metivier had a crucial impact on my academic and personal development. I now have more courage when it comes to using my memory to learn difficult words."

Sventlana Borodina

Individual training is $150 for four one-hour sessions. For booking information, send an email request to rhizomatic@zoho.com

Coming soon from Anthony Metivier

**Relax & Remember
12 Secret Keys to Building Effective Memory Palaces
That Last Forever**

If you have learned the basics of mnemonics, but still struggle to build Memory Palaces, this incredibly in-depth guide to using the power of relaxation to memorize gives an amazing amount of detail on everything you need to know to overcome the fear and doubt many people have about their memories.

With *Relax and Remember* you will learn:

- How to build Memory Palaces the right way
- How the basics of breathwork improve the intensity of your imagination
- Which Hold and Release exercises EVERYONE serious about memorization must know how and when to use
- How to use the 9 Principles of Systema Breathing to release fear and frustration while memorizing
- How to optimize control over and increase the speed of recall

Plus many more tricks and tips that will make your Memory Palaces beautiful, effective and … unforgettable!

As a value added bonus, Anthony interviews several memory experts, including World Memory Champions, doctors, psychologists and teachers. You'll learn from some of the most accomplished memory artists of the present day about the relaxation strategies they couldn't live without when memorizing for fun, pleasure and competition.

© 2012 Metivier Magnetic Memory Series.

All Rights Reserved. No part of this publication may be reproduced in any form or by any means, including scanning, photocopying, or otherwise without prior written permission of the copyright holder.

Disclaimer and Terms of Use: The Author and Publisher have strived to be as accurate and complete as possible in the creation of this book, notwithstanding the fact that he does not warrant or represent at any time that the contents within are accurate due to the rapidly changing nature of the Internet. While all attempts have been made to verify information provided in this publication, the Author and Publisher assumes no responsibility for errors, omissions, or contrary interpretation of the subject matter herein. Any perceived slights of specific persons, peoples, or organizations are unintentional.

This Edition, Copyright 2012

Created in Cyberspace

Printed in Great Britain
by Amazon.co.uk, Ltd.,
Marston Gate.